FATHER LUCIEN GALTIER

1812-1866

LUCIEN GALTIER

PIONEER PRIEST

BY

MARIANNE LUBAN

Copyright © 2011 by Marianne Luban

Second Edition, New and Revised

All rights reserved

Luban, Marianne
Lucien Galtier, Pioneer Priest

ISBN: 978-0-9729524-6-0

Includes index

Printed in the United States
Pacific Moon Publications
PO Box 636
Ogden, Utah 84402

Cover design by Myra R. Jensen.
Cover images from the Minnesota Historical Society Collections, including "Fort Snelling", by Henry Lewis [1819-1904], oil, ca. 1850.

IN MEMORY OF MY PARENTS
WALTER AND GERTRUDE KRAWCZYK
Who came to Minnesota with nothing
from an Old World ravaged by war
and led happy and successful lives

Cathedral of St. Paul ca. 1915
75 years after it all began....
_____

"To what power or authority this new world will become dependent, after it has arisen from its present uncultivated state, time alone can discover. But as the seat of Empire, from time immemorial has been gradually progressive towards the West, there is no doubt but that at some future period, mighty kingdoms will emerge from these wildernesses, and stately palaces and solemn temples, with gilded spires reaching the skies, supplant the Indian huts, whose only decorations are the barbarous trophies of their vanquished enemies."

                Capt. Jonathan Carver
                Early explorer of the Midwest

Father Lucien Galtier and log chapel   Photo: MHS

INTRODUCTION

The lapsing of 170 years seems but a shrug in time given the long history of the world but sometimes some profound changes can occur in a relatively short period. That is why about a century and a half ago life in America was as different from what it is today so as to seem an alien culture. While in our 21st Century we have an African-American president, that would have been simply inconceivable in the 19th even though a terrible internal war was waged over the right of the black man to his freedom. It was the start of a protracted battle for equality of the various peoples who came to inhabit our nation and those who were indigenous, one which continued long after the war between the North and the South had ended and has yet to reach a universal conclusion in our great land.

Americans of the 19th Century looked, thought, wrote,

and even spoke differently from us and there were certainly far fewer of them. Many of their expressions are now regarded as quaint and even corny. Nobody of today can imagine a recruiting poster exhorting "To Arms!" but these existed in the time of that Civil War.

Had they been able to imagine us, the inhabitants of that era would have been as shocked at our perceived depravity as we are at their intolerant attitudes, the stiff Victorian mentality that saw everything as black or white and had no use for shades of gray. In few other epochs were women more covered up, the female figure more distorted, feminine chastity more carefully considered, scrutinized. Yards of cloth, hoops and bustles caused ladies to resemble sailing vessels that glided along. Whalebone corsets were deliberately laced to the point of unhealthy discomfort in order to achieve the hour-glass figure. A glimpse of an ankle, much less a calf, was considered overexposure and décolleté was left to the women of the demi-monde until a bit of cleavage and bared shoulders became permissible in high society in the latter part of the century. Belles had to be beautiful without benefit of makeup. Photographs of nudes or semi-nudes that seem quite innocuous by present standards were considered the height of eroticism.

There was no dry cleaning as we know it even though wool was worn extensively. Without deodorants, women sewed washable dress-shields into their clothing, often also fashioned from materials that one did not launder like satin and velvet. Men were fortunate if they only smelled like "leather and tobacco". It was a good deal of trouble to take a hot bath as the water needed to be heated up on the stove and the tub used was likely the same one wherein the laundry was boiled. It is astonishing but true that even unto the 1800s, some persons in America and Europe went years without fully immersing their bodies in a bath and others never did since they were born.

Both sexes tended to wear their tresses long during the 19th Century and facial hair was very much in evidence.

Most men sported either a mustache or a beard, if not both. Clean-shaven males were in the minority but it would seem that a hirsute face was not much in vogue among the French ecclesiastics in general. Fussy Empire hairstyles were not unknown among the priests, however, although one, named Lucien Galtier, preferred a simpler cut very popular in America.

People were as quick to judge and condemn one another in the frontier towns as they were in more populated places. In the larger cities, hospitals did not accept girls about to give birth out of wedlock, so that they might not outrage, by their presence, the respectability of the staidly married. Regardless, most children were born at home and, although 19th Century medicine remained largely primitive, house calls by doctors were the norm. The physician, however, washed his hands after an operation or procedure and not before.

Any man over the age of fifty was considered "old", without question and, certainly, the subject of this book, Father Galtier, who lived only to the age of fifty-four, was described as being in his "old age" prior to his death. Women, it may be supposed, were no longer thought young from the day they "lost their bloom"—began to show the first signs of aging. Unless the women were well-to-do, that aging process was accelerated by unrelenting toil.

Virtually none of the conveniences we take for granted today were around then. Thomas Edison was not to invent the light bulb until years after the Civil War had ended in 1865 and the horse remained the primary means of getting about. Everything was very much more difficult, even where bodily functions were concerned. Inventors had devised versions of the "water closet" but few people on the frontier had one because it was necessary to be hooked up to a sewage system for it to be practical. And this is merely the tip of the iceberg as to how much the 19th Century differed from the present.

Many of the Roman Catholic clergy of our era would

have difficulty identifying with the mindset of the pioneer priests, the missionaries. By the 1940s, a full century later, it seems evident that America's ideal padre was one Father O'Malley as portrayed by crooner Bing Crosby in the movies. Father O'Malley was tolerant, thoroughly modern, avuncular, and even "savvy". Hellfire and brimstone were not in his arsenal when it came to persuading the errant. The sidewalks of New York would have seemed a great environment to the cinematic priest, a far cry from the observation of Dominican missionary Fr.[1] Samuel Mazzuchelli, upon his landing in the New World, that the size of the city was in direct proportion to the evils therein. The priest was only in his twenties at the time. Mazzuchelli was an Italian from Milan but his French counterparts considered their own capital, Paris, a veritable Babylon, as well.

The pioneer priests and their superiors were, for the most part, proselytizers and, by the same token, passionately religious. They were far more than merely devout and tended to be harsh in their assessments of matters not conforming to their rigid standards. While this aspect of their characters was thought perfectly unremarkable in their day by the white man, the novel *Black Robe*[2] by Brian Moore effectively conveys how strange and even ludicrous the French Jesuits, foremost among the missionaries, and their religion seemed in the eyes of the Indians 200 years before Galtier. This probably still held true more immediately to some extent—although by the 19th Century the natives of the Midwest were becoming accustomed to the ways of the whites very quickly. By that time, they were far more amenable to accepting the theology of the pale faces, especially since quite often the hungry Indians benefited by the generosity of certain denominations.

---

1 Although, in reality, ordinary Catholic priests were referred to as "Mister" in those days.
2 Dutton, 1997, etc.

To Lucien Galtier and the other pioneer priests, Native Americans were souls to be saved, barbarians to be enlightened by the conversion to Christianity. The noble appearance of certain individual tribesmen may have impressed the clerics, but Native American culture never did. It was not respected because it was not considered "respectable" or, rather, moral. The open ways of the woodland Indians, especially with regard to sexuality, scandalized the highly repressed, puritanical abbés. Due to being appalled that the Dakota and Ojibway placed such a low value on human life, it strikes one ironic that the French, fresh from their bloody revolution, mostly referred to them as *les sauvages*.

As condescending as their outlook strikes one today, one must keep in mind that these priests did, in fact, endure tremendous hardships in the service of their God and their deep convictions. They were nothing if not sincere and extraordinarily willing. That the Indians already had a belief system in place was well known to some of them but, even so, it would not have been the proper path to heaven in their opinion.

Their attitudes toward other faiths was also quite typical for the day, if offensive to us. Protestants were the enemy of "the one true church", never mind that they were also Christians. Their missionaries were the avowed rivals of the pioneer priests and even Father Galtier unfortunately wrote: *"The Protestant ministers are numerous...they have one visitant or inspector among them. He might be called the instrument of the spirit of falsehood. They are spendthrifts and appear deferential in order to win converts..."*

But each man, to a great extent, must be viewed within the context of the time in which he existed and the society that formed him. This, above all, the reader must keep in mind. The priests, moreover, were the products of extremely religious families of the kind that tend to provide more than merely one young person for the seminaries and convents. While Lucien Galtier was still in one seminary, his elder brother was already a superior at another. His nephew also seems to have become a priest.

The uncivilized half of the American continent doubtless held the promise of adventure for an eager young Frenchman like Galtier in addition to the opportunity to propagate the faith in which he so fiercely believed. But adventure is a trek into the unknown, the unexpected. And the unforeseen, of course, has a way of becoming ones life.

Father Lucien Galtier, I suspect, resembled Moore's 17th Century Laforgue, the Black Robe, not a little in character and was no less sincere or enthusiastic than his peers. Unlike Laforgue, however, Galtier evidenced little interest in converting the Indians or in learning their languages. That aspect of the ministry he seems to have left to people like his friend, Father Augustin Ravoux. Galtier proved to be an unusual type of missionary. Moreover, he refused to be perpetually long-suffering [he certainly suffered!] and demanded his rights as a person. Galtier clearly did not view himself as an expendable sacrifice to the cause. He was a man who knew his own worth and became troubled when he thought his talents were being wasted. He did not shrink from his duty, as he saw it, but preferred to do it with a modicum of dignity. Comfort, of course, was out of the question, but the sheer deprivation Galtier faced year after year seemed to him in aid of nothing but the breaking of the spirit. This he attempted to convey to his bishop, Mathias Loras, who, although far from luxuriating in wealth, resided in an adequate brick house at Dubuque in Iowa, and usually had enough to eat. But the cries emanating from the wilderness were in vain.

This little work will try to paint the portrait of a seemingly complex personality on a more intimate level than has previously been done. One receives the impression, upon reading other histories of the pioneer priests, that a too-close scrutiny of them was avoided in order to refrain from casting doubt on their "saintly" aspect. Where the tone of the letters of Lucien Galtier to his superior could not be overlooked, he was characterized as "embittered", even to "the point of madness", suggesting Galtier had no right to demand any sort of reasonable treatment for himself and his colleagues.

Being a person who participates but little in organized religion, the present author does not claim to fully understand Lucien Galtier or anybody like him. In fact, I admit I cannot because of the great differences in our basic philosophies. On the other hand, I have no difficulty admiring his courage and contributions and believe he deserves a much-delayed biography just as he merited a park, street, and buildings named after him, a gap that I humbly strive to fill inasmuch as I am able.

While there can be no question that Lucien Galtier was one of the founding fathers of St. Paul, Minnesota, and certainly gave the city its name, this book will not attempt to be a comprehensive chronicle of either the city or the state. That has been admirably accomplished by other writers, notably J. Fletcher Williams, to whose seminal work, *A History of St. Paul to 1875*[3], I am much indebted. The same can be said of Prairie du Chien and Peter Scanlan's *Prairie du Chien: French, British, American*[4] has provided excellent background there.

I am also indebted to those historians who have taught me what history means, that it is reconstructed from conjecture, "the historic imagination", as well as facts and has been ever since Herodotus. A man of note has two lives, the second beginning only when he goes to his grave, that is his life in the memory of others, with the historian having the final word. How much the revivification can resemble the first life is subject to many factors, some beyond the chronicler's control. The greater the distance in time between the biographer and the subject, the more

---

3   Minnesota Historical Society Press [St. Paul, 1876].
4   Menasha, Wisc., Collegiate Press [1937].

difficult the task. But one really can make a man come alive again—just a little—and the greatest responsibility is not to make him and his era seem too dull in the process. This writer personally believes that a voice from the past is the one worth listening to if one wishes to know "how things really were" and that is why I have included as many pertinent eyewitness accounts of the frontier as possible.

"Behold, we have left all things and have followed Thee."
[Matt. XIX, 27]

ORIGINS

Lucien Galtier is one of those people whose name is recognized, especially in the Twin Cities, the one great metropolitan area of the state of Minnesota, and also in Prairie du Chien, Wisconsin—but about whom very little is generally known. As a man, he is highly lauded, yet personal anecdotes about him are quite scarce. Some of those who have praised Father Galtier in print cannot have ever met him and had either to imagine the fine qualities they attributed to him or obtained the information second hand.

Even his best remaining likeness, representing what seems to have been Galtier's middle age, defies one to pin down just what is behind those eyes. At first, they appear rather cold, quite severe, but if one stares long enough, the first impression fades and one sees nothing but a melancholy intelligence. We know that Father Galtier wrote eloquently and spiritedly because there are a number of his communications in existence, but his situation afforded him little opportunity to write letters that reveal what he *liked* instead of lamented.

That is, Galtier may have written such letters to someone, a friend or family member, but they have either been lost forever or no interested party has found them. Only in one extant missive does the priest set down the details of a festive occasion with such enthusiastic delight that one can imagine the eyes shining as the pen moved across the paper. But that letter still exists only thanks to church bureaucracy and not because someone cherished it or expected the author to become a figure of history. Even the priest probably never foresaw it, although there is some evidence that he perhaps hoped to be more prominent than he was in his chosen field at one time. That hope never came to fruition while the man lived, although when a bishop asked him to put down some recollections, some experiences, of his youth, Galtier may have realized his name was not going to fade into nothingness, after all. If so, what prevented him from giving a fuller auto- biographical account of himself? Why was he so brief? That, like so much about Lucien Galtier, is impossible to fathom.

Regarding the birthplace of Father Galtier, an unaccountable error has long been accepted as fact. Archbishop John Ireland of St. Paul, who added his comments to the afore-mentioned memoir of the priest,[5] represented him as hailing from the département of Ardèche in southern France, and has him pursuing his ecclesiastical studies in his native diocese. The biographical data of the Archdiocese of Dubuque for Galtier states that he was born in the Ardèche, "diocese of Rodez", but the names Ardèche and Rodez do not go together. Even Galtier's superior, Bishop Mathias Loras, describes him in a letter as being from Rodez and, in another, from the "diocese of Rodez", which is actually in the département of Aveyron.[6] Moreover, while Ireland maintained that Lucien

---

5 *Memoir of Rev. Lucian Galtier: the first Catholic priest of Saint Paul* by Rev. John Ireland, [1880]. In reality, "Lucien" is the correct version and the entire memoir, as printed, is only eighteen pages in length. Because the priest usually signed his communications as "L. Galtier", some did not know how to spell the first name. As to the vocalization of the surname, it is "Gal-tee-ey".

6 After the Revolution, France was segmented into 83 departments.

Galtier was born in 1811, his tomb at Prairie du Chien, Wisconsin, bears the date of December 17, 1812. In 1801, the diocese of Rodez was suppressed and merged with the diocese of Cahors and the diocese of Saint-Flour—not to be restored as an autonomous diocese until 1817. Therefore, it becomes clear that during the years 1811-1812, when Galtier was purportedly born, there was no "diocese of Rodez" in existence. In one of his letters to Loras, Galtier mentioned having been at the seminary of Rodez at the time he elected to go to America, so Loras may have connected him to Rodez because that is where he obtained him.

    Even though the two départements are not very distant from each other, Galtier would never have claimed to be from the Ardèche had he been born anywhere even close to the city of Rodez, which is a major urban center of the Aveyron. So whence Ardèche? What seems odd is that there should have been a mystery here at all and that the prelate of Dubuque did not record even such minimal correct personal data about all of the priests serving in his diocese that there can be no question as to their natal date and place. In any case, someone began the connection of Father Galtier to the Ardèche—but it is not likely Galtier, himself, can have been that source.

    The truth is that the priest was born in a town called St. Affrique in the département of Aveyron.[7] What is now the département of Aveyron was once the ancient province of Rouergue, which was not far from the northern part of the old division of Languedoc. The provinces of the kingdom of France were rather vague as to their boundaries and the territories were defined by tradition. Today, when people refer to the old provinces or divisions, they actually refer to what existed in 1789—before the new government following the Revolution abolished the divisions and created the départements with their well-defined limits. Regardless,

---

7 Last Will and Testament of Rev. Lucien Galtier, on file in the courthouse of Crawford County, Wisconsin.

anybody in the southern part of the nation still knows what is meant by "Rouergue" and "Languedoc". [8]

Seminary at Rodez, France

It seems likely that the distant forebears of Lucien Galtier really did originate in that division of Languedoc and, by northbound migration, become associated with Rouergue. Languedoc is known to be the ancestral home of the Gaud family, the numerous variants of the name including Gauthé, Gauthier and Galtier. The region of Languedoc encompasses the southeastern portion of the Massif Central, a plateau in the south of France, to the Rhone river. It was annexed to France in 1271 under King Louis IX. Thus is Languedoc described:

"This was Languedoc [12th century] the real mix of people, the true Babel. Located at the bend of the highway from France, Spain and Italy, it had a singular fusion of Iberian, Gallic, Roman, and Gothic blood. These diverse elements are formed out of harsh opposition. There was to be the great battle of beliefs and races. What beliefs? I would gladly say all [...] The Semitic element, Jew and Arab, was strong in Languedoc. Narbonne had long been the

---

8   A dialect called Occitan was spoken there.

capital of the Saracens in France. The Jews were innumerable. Abused, but still suffered, they flourished in Carcassonne, Montpellier, Nimes, their rabbis holding public schools there. They formed a link between Christians and Moslems, between France and Spain..."

Jules Michelet , *Histoire de France* , 1861

The walled city of Carcassonne

There was a certain Deodat de Galtier who was prominent in Rouergue in 1250 and Guillaume de Galtier of St. Affrique was awarded the title Knight of Malta in 1499 for his courage in battle. Circa 1692, Pierre de Galtier, Seigneur de Montagnol, served as a Counselor of the King and Judge of St. Affrique. Other branches of the family dropped the "de" and became ordinary citizens of the town, although often adhering to the professions of the law and medicine. Due to the difficulty of accessing birth records from outside of France, I am unable to vouch for those of the priest at this time,[9] nor does the young Galtier fully materialize for our purposes until he reaches the north-

---

9   However, see page 194 for second-hand information I received from a French genealogist.

American continent. The family name, in its oldest version, Gaud, has a Germanic etymology, deriving from "waldan" or "governor". A certain St. Gaud was also called "Waldus", for example. At any rate, whatever its original ethnicity, the Gaud/Gauthier/Galtier clan was thought to be seated in Languedoc since ancient times with manors, lands, and a crest and coat of arms. The oldest known coat of arms for the family was a red band with six blackbirds on a gold background. The crest was a black eagle and the motto was "*A chacun sa vue*" with the meaning "To each his own vision".

As has been noted, a number of lords and illustrious persons arose from the various branches of the family, with the surname having undergone its spelling changes over time depending upon who wrote it. The name "Galtier" is widespread in the département of Aveyron. It may even be that Father Lucien Galtier was not the first of his many distant relatives to come to America and there is some evidence to support this supposition.

Doubtless, the Galtier family had its varieties of ethnic infusion, as well. There had been Romans in Languedoc and also Vandals, Sueves, Visigoths and Franks. When someone wrote that Lucien Galtier had "the face of a Caesar", he may have unwittingly perceived that a bit of Latin blood did, indeed, course through the priest's veins, the souvenir of some legion's occupation. But nothing of the kind can be known for certain without the unlikely sequencing of Galtier's DNA. Judging from his extant likenesses, Galtier appears to have had dark eyes and curling dark-brown or black hair. No matter what the circumstances of his more immediate fathers had been, there was nothing of the peasant in the features or demeanor of Galtier. He was every inch the aristocrat, one person having gone so far as to have observed "*his head sat upon his shoulders like a military chieftain*".[10] And,

---

10 Newson, Thomas, *Pen Pictures of Minnesota and Biographical Sketches of Old Settlers* [St. Paul, 1886].

ultimately, battle he did—with everything unfavorable to the well-being of Man—like some young Don Quixote of the prairies with the odds firmly stacked against him.

Even the origin of the name of St. Affrique is in doubt but the local tradition has it that St. Africanus, bishop of Comminges, being persecuted by the Visigoths in 470 AD, sought refuge in a place called Vicaria Curiensis by the Romans. This location then became St. Affrique, which is not attested until the year 942, however. At the time Father Galtier died, some of his immediate family was still living in and around St. Affrique. The priest, himself, owned land there, as had his father before him.

BISHOP MATHIAS LORAS

A son of another very religious but far better documented family was Lucien Galtier's superior, the Right Reverend Mathias Loras. Born in Lyons in the year 1792, [the tenth of eleven children] the father, two brothers and two sisters of Pierre-Jean-Mathias fell under the blade of the guillotine at the time of the French Revolution. This left the bishop's mother and her remaining offspring in greatly diminished circumstances. Mathias, the first name he went by, was ordained in 1815 and in 1829, at the age of 37, he left for America. When he was 45 he was elevated to the position of the first prelate of the newly-created diocese of Dubuque. We will see much more of the name of Loras in this book because this man's relationship with Galtier was a crucial one. It is difficult to judge, from a distance of so many decades, how well-disposed Bishop Loras truly was toward his charge. However, the ultimate verdict must be, in the instant opinion—"not very".

Mathias Loras arrived in New York in 1838 from a trip to France, accompanied by two priests and four subdeacons, all volunteers for his proposed missions. They had departed from Le Havre on the American brig *Lion* with eleven other missionaries for different dioceses. Also on board was the body of St. Cessianus, presented to Loras for relics by Pope Gregory XVI. The names of the priests were Cretin and Pelamourgues and the subdeacons, eventually ordained, were Galtier, Ravoux, Causse, and Petiot. These last four were given over to St. Mary's College and Seminary at Emmitsburg, Maryland, for their continued studies, now to include English. Loras had high hopes of all of them in the beginning, but it becomes evident, from his correspondence[11] of the ensuing years, that he favored Lucien Galtier the least and perhaps Joseph Cretin, future bishop of St. Paul, Minnesota, the most. Joseph Cretin was already known to Loras, as the former had been his student when he taught at the seminary of Meximieux in their homeland.

The Diocese of Dubuque encompassed what was then the Territory of Iowa, the present State of Iowa, and Minnesota. Parts of Wisconsin and Illinois were also involved. At the time of its founding, the unfinished church of St. Raphael at Dubuque was the only Catholic church

---

11 *Foundations: The Letters of Mathias Loras, D.D. Bishop of Dubuque*, transcribed, translated, and edited by Robert Klein, assisted by Sr. Benvenuta Bras, O.P. [Loras College Press, Dubuque, 2004] is the source of some of the bishop's outgoing correspondence in this work. Some of the incoming mail has *Letters to a Pioneer Bishop, Correspondence to Mathias Loras, D.D., First Bishop of Dubuque*, edited by Rev. Loras Otting [Loras College Press, Dubuque, 2009] as its source. Translation from the French in the present book is by M. Luban.

within the boundaries of the diocese and the Rev. Samuel Mazzuchelli, its pastor, the only Catholic priest. Mazzuchelli, although a Dominican missionary, accepted Mathias Loras as his bishop and their association continued for a number of fruitful years. Mazzuchelli had left Italy for the American missions in 1828.

If others had agreed with Loras' apparently not very great opinion of Galtier, that might be more readily understandable, but Lucien rarely failed to impress in other quarters. This epitaph seems to sum it up: *"Father Galtier was a man of remarkable personality and power; he had the face of a Caesar and the heart of a Madonna; in him strength and tenderness, culture and simplicity, met and mingled in the formation of a noble character. If he had remained in France, his talents and his virtues would have marked him for high honors, but he preferred the rugged lot and privations of pioneer life to the power and fame for which petty men strive."*[12]

How could Bishop Loras fail to esteem such a paragon as described above? One can't be sure, but imagination is not powerless to speculate that perhaps Galtier was too perfect for Mathias Loras in some respects and far too strong in others. Without a doubt, Galtier was a truly handsome person, well proportioned, with very fine eyes and, perhaps, in the opinion of Loras, he really did hold that striking head on his shoulders a bit too high. If another, some years later, described Lucien as "elegant", that may not have been lost on the bishop, as well.

Can it really be maintained that a woman or a man who has been blessed with an above average appearance has no idea of it? Perhaps he or she does not know the full extent of the blessing [for no one sees himself as others do] but, over some years, remarks, compliments, and admiring

---

12 McNulty, Rev. Ambrose, *The Chapel of St. Paul and the Beginnings of the Catholic Church In Minnesota* [1905], and *Acta et Dicta*, Vol. I, The St. Paul Historical Society, July 1907. Father McNulty had spoken with at least one individual who had known Galtier personally.

glances will assure one that something admirable exists. Perhaps, then, Galtier, although surely aspiring to avoid all the seven deadly sins, at very least could not avoid drawing eyes to him. Was it possible Bishop Loras feared that Galtier was too attractive? After all, Lucien was an unknown quantity at the start of their association and Loras, being well aware of how certain ladies cannot resist fawning over a handsome priest, may have worried that the young man would be subjected to temptation. Although Lucien was sent to a place where there were few women and scarcely any white ones at all, so were the other priests of the diocese—to varying extents. They went into a kind of exile in some backwoods or another, maintaining contact with civilization only via the sporadic mail service depending upon the riverboats and a few intrepid couriers. Still, there were some isolated instances of Loras' men not being able to control all their impulses.

That the 19th Century French publicly acknowledged priests were not to be confused with angels, had their human frailties, with some even having taken Holy Orders for the wrong reasons, is exemplified by the hugely popular opera, *Manon,* by Jules Massenet. Its hero, Des Grieux, becomes a priest on account of disappointment in love and life but his former lover, Manon, has little difficulty persuading him to return to her when she decides to try. While nobody could claim surprise at any goings-on in Paris, on the stage or off, priests of the American frontier towns cultivated even platonic women friends at their own peril.

One such case revolved around a Belgian contemporary of Galtier, Father Florimond J. Bonduel, a flute-playing cleric who had a knack for drawing controversy to him. Father Bonduel was accused of conducting an affair with Mrs. Rosalie Dousman, a widow with several children, who taught girls in the tiny parochial school at a location known as "Shanty Town", three miles north of Green Bay in Wisconsin.

John Dousman Jr., occupation farmer and trader, had

married Rosalie, nee LaBorde, at Mackinac, Michigan. Rosalie, who had been born in 1796 in the same place she was wed and died in 1872 at Green Bay, devoted much of her life to instructing youngsters and was hardly of a flighty disposition. However, her path paralleled that of Father Bonduel from Mackinac Island to Lake Poygan, Keshena and, finally, Green Bay.

← Rosalie Dousman in old age[13]

Bonduel, himself not born until 1799, was a missionary who served in first the Detroit diocese and then in that of Milwaukee.[14] The priest was incensed by these allegations regarding himself and Rosalie to the point of threatening legal action against the rumor mongers. Mrs. Dousman was a Catholic teacher under his supervision—in fact the only female instructor—there being as yet no nuns in the area. Certainly, she and Bonduel were on friendly terms and why not?

The busybodies were forced to apologize but Father Bonduel was not comfortable remaining where he was and left on a trip to Europe. Bonduel could be temperamental. Once, fed up with the Menominee Indians at his mission, he chopped down a wooden cross he had erected on a hill near their encampment, having temporarily concluded they did not deserve to have a priest among them.

---

13 Wisconsin Historical Society , image #71567
14 In fact, Father Bonduel was the initial priest ordained in the diocese of Detroit in 1834. His first mission was that of St. Ann's on Mackinac Island until 1838. Bonduel has a town named for him in eastern WI. The priest served as pastor of St. John the Evangelist, Green Bay, until his death on December 13, 1861. He is buried in Allouez Cemetery.

Father Florimond J. Bonduel

Bonduel eventually returned to Green Bay, serving the missions of the vicinity until his death. And yet, in the end, the priest willed all his personal belongings to Rosalie Dousman, including his silver watch and flute. Perhaps Father Bonduel really had been more than a little fond of the widow—or he could think of no one else in America who would have any sentimental interest in this property of no great value, all that remained of his earthly existence.[15]

Samuel Mazzuchelli's description of a lady who must have been Mrs. Dousman renders any hanky panky even more unlikely: In his eyes she was *"that zealous and prudent person...mistress of the Menominee language[16] and familiar with both English and French..."*

Rosalie was, in addition, a talented craftsperson as evidenced by a very nicely decorated birchbark maple sugar container, an artifact owned by the Wisconsin Historical Society. It is interesting that there was, among Bonduel's effects, a note from a Father Jean Claude Perrodin, indicating the latter owed him eighty dollars. The connection of Lucien Galtier to these two men will become apparent before long and the name Dousman is one with which he would ultimately become very familiar. Did Galtier, himself, eventually forge a bond with a capable woman whose good qualities he admired? The answer must be "yes".

It is amazing how the lives of the pioneer priests in the missions of the Midwest intersected, they being at some point in one diocese and then another, moving here and there. They relieved one another at some post, served together briefly, or merely met on travels. They may have corresponded, not actually seeing one another for years. All

---

15 The probate court valued the items at $492.18, but how much Mrs. Dousman actually received is unrecorded. Source: *Florimond J. Bonduel, Missionary to Wisconsin Territory* by Malcolm Rosholt and Msgr. John Britten Gehl, [Wisconsin, 1976].

16 Doubtless Mazzuchelli was right about this but Rosalie had grown up with Chippewa, her grandmother having been of this nation. Later, Mrs. Dousman had received a formal education in Quebec.

seemed to know what the others were up to, thought about their superiors, and, despite the lack of instant communication, rumors flew about. The fathers were, after all, a kind of army, soldiers of Christ, regardless of being in religious orders or diocesan priests. They were interested in each others endeavors and, above all, did not want to feel any more alone than they already were. The abbés did not all like one another—far from it—but if one of their own couldn't be touched for a few dollars now and then, who could be? One had to be above asking a parish member for a personal loan and money from home [Europe] could be a long time in arriving.

Not the slightest breath of scandal has ever been attached to the name of Lucien Galtier in Minnesota but, in the small town where he last lived, there may have been some puzzled speculation. At any rate, a homily that he authored indicates a reluctance to even look at a woman, especially a beautiful, young one. In his other writings, he usually mentions only those who were safely married.

"Listen also to this advice of the Holy Ghost, by the mouth of Ecclesiasticus: 'Gaze not upon a maiden, lest her beauty be a stumbling block to thee. Turn thy face from a woman dressed up, and gaze not upon another's beauty. For many have perished by the beauty of a woman and hereby lust is enkindled as a fire.'"[17]

One way or another, Galtier's first assignment to a tiny settlement where intemperance was rampant may have had some point—other than the fact that Loras had so few priests to send anywhere. Pelamourgues went to Davenport, Petiot was sent to Galena, Illinois, to help Mazzuchelli, and Ravoux was soon dispatched to Prairie du Chien, Wisconsin. Causse found himself at a place called Snake Diggings, later Potosi, also in Wisconsin. Cretin was appointed to Prairie du Chien in time, but, before that, Loras kept him at Dubuque to educate the young men who had not yet been ordained,

---

17 From Galtier's "On Modesty", included in "*Reminiscences, Memoirs and Lectures of Monsignor A. Ravoux, VG*", [St. Paul, 1890].

they having been recalled from Maryland. Galtier and the others were admitted to the priesthood on January 5, 1840 and it would appear that he was the last of the new clergy to receive a position.

There were many more Catholics [700, according to one source] in and around Prairie du Chien than near Fort Snelling because the former was a far older settlement. Bishop Loras could have posted Galtier there, but elected to send the less-prepossessing Ravoux, instead.

Should the reader's interest happen to be piqued by the designation "Snake Diggings", Mazzuchelli provides a description in his autobiography[18] *"...it will not be out of place here to make mention of the first establishment of the Catholic Church in the place called in English, Snake Hollow, that is in Italian Scavi del serpente. About fifteen miles from the southern boundary line of Wisconsin, there is a valley three miles in length, terminating at the Mississippi River. During the War with the Indians in 1832,[19] a cave was discovered here containing a great number of rattlesnakes; on this account when they began to dig there in search of lead, the place was called Snake Hollow. The lead mines in this part of the Territory being very rich, many flocked there in search of the precious metal, and in this manner many settlements were made in the valley under various names; the principal one at present where trade is centered is called Potosi, situated about three miles from the River."*

As Bishop Loras had visited Fort Snelling and what had grown up around it [for wherever soldiers are stationed

---

18 Mazzuchelli, Samuel Charles, *Memoirs Historical and Edifying of a Missionary Apostolic of the Order of St. Dominic Among Various Indian Tribes and Among Catholics and Protestants in the United States of America* [Chicago, 1915]. Translated from the Italian original by Sister Mary Benedicta, O.P., of St. Clara Convent, Sisinawa, Wis.

19 The Black Hawk War.

others come to cater to their vices, even encourage them], had been there before Galtier, he was certainly not ignorant of the disadvantages of the area. One of these was the ancient conflict between the Dakota and Ojibway, which could erupt in bloodshed at any time.

"During the month of June, 1839, there came to Fort Snelling over twelve hundred Chippewas thinking that there they would be paid their annuities for the land they had ceded in 1837. There were two main groups—one which came down from the headwaters of the Mississippi, and the other which came up the river from the vicinity of the St. Croix. At the same time Sioux numbering eight hundred and seventy were encamped near the agency. This was considered an opportune time to conclude a peace, and so the long calumet with its mixture of tobacco and bark of the willow tree was smoked while friendly athletic contests were held on the prairie. On July 1st the two parties of Chippewas started for home. But in one of the bands were the two sons of the man who had been murdered the year before. In the evening before beginning their homeward journey, they visited the graveyard of the fort to cry over the grave of their father. Here the thought of vengeance came to them, and morning found them hidden in the bushes near the trail that skirted the shore of Lake Harriet. The Badger, a Sioux warrior, was the first to pass that way as he went out in the early morning to hunt pigeons. A moment later he was shot and scalped. The murderers then hurried away and hid behind the water at Minnehaha Falls. A few hours later, when the news had spread throughout all the Sioux villages, two bands set out to take revenge upon the departing Chippewas. The old men, the women, and the children remained at home, eagerly awaiting the result of the coming battle and cutting their arms and legs with their knives in grief over the losses which they knew their bands would have to undergo.

It happened that at that time the Right Reverend Mathias Loras, the first Bishop of Dubuque, was at Fort

Snelling. *He had been an interested spectator at the Sioux-Chippewa peace parleys, had watched the departure of the determined avengers, and now was anxiously awaiting the result of the conflict. On the morning of July 4th as he was praying at his altar for the prosperity of his country he was startled by the shrill notes of the Sioux death-song, and gazing through the window saw a bloody throng, dancing about the long poles from which dangled scalps with parts of the skulls still attached. Two terrible struggles had taken place the day before. On the Rum River seventy Chippewa scalps had been taken, and on the banks of Lake St. Croix twenty-five more were obtained. In both cases the losses of the Sioux were smaller. These trophies were brought to the villages, where they were danced about nightly until the leaves began to fall in the autumn, when they were buried.*"[20]

    As there was probably nothing about Lucien that would have prompted the bishop to believe he was especially suited to dealing with drunkards or feuding natives, he may have been sent up-river to teach him humility or, to be fair, what Loras might have perceived as its lack. Or some sort of lesson the reason for which may never be known.

    If so, did it work? Not entirely. But one thing is certain. The memoir of Galtier—what there is of it—makes it plain that the young, newly-ordained diocesan cleric had not been properly apprised by his bishop as to how bad the situation really was. That he only learned when he arrived at his post on the St. Peter River.[21] While on the subject of Father Galtier's character where humility is concerned, let it be stated here that no one we know of ever accused the priest of being anything but modest—except Loras. In fact,

---

20 Hansen, Marcus L., *Old Fort Snelling 1819-1858* [Iowa City, 1918].
21 The old name for the Minnesota.

his modesty was noted, as we have seen, but that may have been achieved with time. Life is a great teacher and Galtier's own was nothing if not a humbling experience. Still, we are left to wonder how effective Loras felt Galtier would be at St. Peter's. Unlike his colleague, Ravoux, Lucien was not making great strides with the Sioux language and did not dwell among the Dakota as their teacher. As a matter of fact, there were so few actual Catholics in the vicinity of Fort Snelling that Galtier had to become an itinerant minister and was never a full-time resident of St. Paul, being based mainly at Mendota.

People are given to saying that a wilderness has a certain purity of balance, is a perfect work of creation. Perhaps that is true, but wherever there are men, they will find a way to sully it, for that seems to be their nature. Stripped of the trappings of civilization, their baser instincts can come to the fore. Men can become coarse, even wild, in order to insure their survival. They become one with the wilderness, and often learn to be as cunning as the natives they find there so that the latter will not overcome them. Hardship deadens the heart, empties the soul. A wilderness is lonely and it is the solitude that is the most destructive of all, for few men prefer it, seek it out. In order to flourish in an environment that consists only of what nature provides, one must be born there. Or be a little mad. One cannot miss what one never had. Otherwise, one must long, every day, for those comforts to which one had been accustomed all ones life and feel an endless sense of deprivation, though one might beg God for serenity and acceptance.

Galtier never grew coarse, was never described as cunning, could hardly be wild, but the change that took place in him in order to survive can be seen in his letters. Judging by the correspondence, it becomes clear over time that Lucien Galtier did not have the disposition of an ascetic monk, one who views privation as the road to sanctity. He was not enamored of the idea of becoming a holy martyr. What he became was angry.

But there is one particular other thing about a wilderness. A man can learn about himself there much more quickly than in cities and towns containing distractions of every sort. Galtier, being engaged in God's work and not needing to toil with his hands [although he was forced to now and then] or wrack his brain for the means to turn a profit, had more time than most to contemplate his own heart.

Despite initially seeking adventure due to the romantic, poetic, soul that emerges in some of his letters, the priest came to realize that he was not suited to the life of a missionary among indigenous peoples or indifferent whites but preferred to minister to those who were already committed Catholics. Galtier was willing to work hard, endure much, on behalf of the faithful, but a proselytizer he was not inclined to be. This, probably more than anything else, earned him the scorn of Mathias Loras, who wanted self-effacing trailblazers and not priests who would have been better off remaining in Europe among their own if they expected a decent lifestyle. Galtier never stopped making demands, insisted upon reminding the bishop with his pen, powered by a wonderful and vivid command of the French language, how wretchedly the missionaries existed. When Loras made promises he would not or could not keep, Galtier found that unacceptable. But we are getting too far ahead. We must go back to the beginning, the time when Lucien Galtier first set foot in what was to become the Minnesota Territory.[22]

---

22 Not until 1849, but the states will henceforth simply be called by their names regardless of when they became territories or achieved statehood.

PIG'S EYE LANDING

It is now regarded as a humorous thing that the large city of St. Paul was once known mostly as the haunt of a man with the squint of a pig, a purveyor of whiskey, no less. But first came the fort, the building of which commenced in 1820 and was completed in 1825, being named after its commanding officer, Col. Josiah Snelling. Fort Snelling still stands today atop a bluff at the point where the Mississippi and Minnesota rivers meet. It commands a wonderfully picturesque view, looking toward the rivers. From the heights of the fort, one can still see the waters and wooded areas as they must have appeared to Lucien Galtier. The same pathway that led him from the shore below to its gates is still there. There is even a small plot of carefully cultivated prairie at the fort, amid which wildflowers show their delicate pastels in the summer. But to imagine this prairie stretching out mile after mile, an ocean of grasses and flowers, is no longer so easy.

Across the Minnesota from the garrison is what is now called Mendota but what was originally referred to as St. Peter's. On the opposite side of the Mississippi from the fort is the old part of St. Paul. In the midst of it all is Pike Island. Once completed, the fort had a rather nice house for the commander, officer's quarters, barracks for the enlisted men, a hospital, guardhouse, general store that provided goods the army did not issue, and eventually a schoolhouse and a stone chapel—not to mention all those things that properly belong to an outpost that might have to defend itself from onslaught. That never happened, but Fort Snelling, once it no longer had the capacity of protecting the fur trade or controlling the Indians, became a training center for troops in conflicts from the Civil War to World War II.

The fortress received its supplies via steamboats traveling up the Mississippi during the navigable seasons [the river froze in winter], but hundreds of loaves of bread were baked on site each day. A blacksmith, carpenter, wheelwright, and armorer were necessary in order to maintain the weapons and every sort of paraphernalia in the environs of Fort Snelling.

At Mendota was the headquarters of the American Fur Company, founded by John Jacob Astor, a considerable enterprise with its own army of trappers and traders.[23]

An Indian agent, Maj. Lawrence Taliaferro, was appointed by the United States government to oversee the dealings with the Sioux and Chippewa[24] tribes of the area. These two nations had not been on good terms as far back as anyone could recall and the objective was to keep peace between them. Assisting Taliaferro was the local interpreter, Scott Campbell, very proficient in the Indian tongues, in addition to French and English, being the son of a Scotsman and a Sioux woman. He had been born at Prairie du Chien in 1790. Campbell was, himself, allied with a half-breed[25] of the Menominee tribe and resided in a house with her and their numerous offspring on the riverbank below the fort. Margaret Campbell was baptized by Bishop Loras on the occasion of his first voyage to St. Peter's and had the reputation of a good woman but just how much Christianity was instilled into some of her nine children will be seen anon.

---

23 The main quarry was beaver pelts, due to beaver hats being de rigueur for gentlemen of fashion.
24 Otherwise known as the Dakota and Ojibway
25 The author is not very comfortable employing this outmoded term, but in the 19th Century it was very commonly used. The French called them *metis*.

Life at Fort Snelling is best described by an eyewitness, an army surgeon, Dr. Nathan Jarvis, who served there from 1833 to 1836.

"As to news, little can occur in this distant region, secluded from the world. We pass our time something in the way of exiles, banish'd from the pleasures and I may add follies of civiliz'd life. Still there are charms even in savage life and the wilderness, as proof of which there are many men in this country acting as Indian traders and possessing talent who after accumulating fortunes by the profits of the trade, marry Indian wives and settle themselves down for life, abandoning any idea of ever returning to the places of their birth or their friends...
My expenses at this post including mess, servant, washing, horse keeping, etc. amount to about $25 a month. My pay is $82 a month and I likewise receive about $100 a year from the Ind. Agent for attending sick Indians and about $100 more from private practice, making in all nearly $1,200 a year.
I have one of the best rooms in the garrison, the hospital range being built of stone. But what is of more importance in this climate and such winters as we have here, is that we received this summer 30 & 40 large stoves for the use of the garrison...The winter usually sets in the beginning of November when everything remains in thick ribb'd ice until nearly the middle of April. What do you think of the thermometer being as low as 30 degrees below zero? Such is the case every winter in this climate...
As to how the Sabbath is observed here, the only way it is known is by a relaxation of the men from their daily fatigue [not garrison duty] and Sunday inspection. Otherwise it is unknown here—

The sound of the church going bell.
These rocks and these valleys ne'er heard....

The officers are very agreeable men, altho' too much addicted to cards, which is the prevailing vice in all these outposts where men are shut out from amusements during the long and severe winters." [letter dated Oct. 10, 1833]

Jarvis also told his sister, Mary, in yet another letter, that the fort library *"contains about 400 vols of excellent books to which is attached a Reading Room which is abundantly suppl'd with Newspapers & Periodicals"*—most being months out of date, of course. It happened in 1834 that *"the soldiers amuse themselves by having Balls in the Fort twice a week...Their partners are mostly those ladies of the garrison...Camp women together with the ladies without [i.e.* outside the garrison, but of unclear status] *If they do not dance with grace they at least make it up in strength & duration, generally continuing from 8 o'clock in the evening until 8 in the morning..."*

This physician mentions nothing about drinking sprees but his successor, Dr. John Emerson, wrote to the Surgeon General of the United States in a letter dated April 23, 1839: *"Since the middle of winter we have become completely inundated with ardent spirits, and consequently the most beastly scenes of intoxication among the soldiers of this garrison and the Indians in its vicinity, which, no doubt, will add many cases to our sick-list. The whiskey is brought here by citizens who are pouring in upon us and settling themselves on the opposite shore of the Mississippi River, in defiance of our worthy commanding officer, Maj. J. Plympton, whose authority they set at naught...Pardon me, sir, if I err in writing so, but I feel grieved to witness such scenes of drunkenness and dissipation where I have spent so many days of happiness, when we had no ardent spirits among us, and, consequently, sobriety and good conduct among the command. May I presume to ask you to use your influence with the proper authorities to mark out the Reserve, and rid us of these harpies or whiskey-sellers who destroy the health of the soldiers..."*

This letter found its way to the Secretary of War and,

although strict and even extreme measures were taken, nothing sufficed to shut down the unlicensed whiskey trade altogether at that time, nor for decades into the future.

Lest one be inclined to think Dr. Emerson may have been exaggerating, the severity of the problem was attested to by others, including the Indian Agent. Maj. Taliaferro made a notation in his diary on June 3, 1839, around the very time that Bishop Loras paid his visit to the site:[26] *"...forty-seven soldiers were confined to the guard-house for drunkenness in one night, having been arrested in an uproarious spree in a whiskey hovel across the river, kept by a man named Mink, who was, for that offense, sent out of the country..."*

Indeed, we see no more about this Mink, but other men kept up a brisk business in what the Indians called *"Minne-wakan"* or *"Powerful Water"*, notably Pierre Parrant with his marble-hued blind eye, and Donald McDonald.

Most chilling of all is the recollection of Mrs. James Patten, who had once lived at Fort Snelling, as her father, Richard Mortimer, had been a commissary sergeant there. Mrs. Patten stated that intoxicated soldiers actually froze to death while trying to climb back up to the fort in winter. Their bodies were eaten by wolves. The more fortunate ones lost feet or hands to frostbite, becoming cripples. Yet the men remained so desperate for the drink that one, a Sergeant Mann, paid eighty dollars for a gallon of whiskey that was not exactly the finest Scotch.[27] Richard Mortimer, one might add, was an Englishman who had even been educated at the prestigious Eton. Upon leaving the army, Mortimer settled in St. Paul and was the first to raise a flag there. He purchased "Old Glory" for thirty-five dollars and had it run up a pole in front of his house. This happened on Christmas, 1842.

But, back in 1839, there was already a man of the

---

26 Loras left Dubuque on June 23.
27 That was quite an expensive jug, recalling that an army surgeon, who surely earned more than a sergeant, made a little over $80. per month.

cloth responsible for the spiritual welfare of the soldiers of Fort Snelling, then a seemingly unenviable job. His name was Rev. Ezekiel Gear, the chaplain, also a missionary. He had come from Galena via Prairie du Chien, where he met with an accident on a sleigh that cost him a lengthy stay at the local Fort Crawford infirmary. Gear arrived at the garrison to the north on April 28 of '39 and continued in his position until 1858, when Fort Snelling was shut down for a while. Reverend Gear retired with all honor to Minneapolis, where he stayed for the rest of his life. He must be included among those who met Father Lucien Galtier and perhaps offered him comfort during a very trying time when he hovered between life and death.

Painting of Fort Snelling by John Casper Wild
Pike Island is in the foreground[28]

---

28 Minnesota Historical Society Collections.

THE TREATIES OF 1837

In this year in Minnesota history, a group of about twenty chiefs and braves of the Dakota and Ojibway traveled to Washington to make a treaty giving up their lands east of the Mississippi to the United States for cash. Before that, all of Minnesota, excepting a small reservation around Fort Snelling, belonged to the Nations and, needless to say, it was not yet a state. The treaties with the tribes opened up the way for agriculture, farmers and more settlers, supposedly without molestation by the Indians. At the time of the ratifications, the only settlers near the fort were some refugees from the Red River area, mainly tillers of the soil, a few Canadian voyageurs, and some men who had left the army. J. Fletcher Williams listed these as being: [in 1838] Pierre "Pigs Eye" Parrant, Abraham Perry, Edward Phelan, William Evans, _____ Johnson, Benjamin Gervais, Pierre Gervais and [in 1839] John Hays, James R. Clewett, Vital Guerin, Denis Cherrier, Charles Mousseau, and William Beaumette. 1840 seems to have seen the advent of Joseph Rondo [or Rondeau].

However, when Bishop Mathias Loras visited the area in 1839, a German language newspaper in Cincinnati called the *Wahrheits-Freund* reported the following:

"At the junction of St. Peter's and the Mississippi rivers—45 degrees northern latitude, and about 2,100 miles from New Orleans—the Americans erected recently a splendid fortress for the protection of the Indian tribes which roam about these localities. The Bishop of Dubuque believing there might be Catholic families at that point, made a voyage up there toward the end of last June. To his great astonishment he found there not far from the fort 185 families, consisting mostly of Indians and French. No pen can describe the joy which this apparently lost flock of the Church manifested, when its members saw this bishop in their midst, since up to this time no priest much less a bishop had advanced up to them. The messengers of heaven now began their course of instruction, which continued for weeks, to prepare their people for the reception of the holy sacraments. Fifty-six children, in addition many adults, whites and reds, received baptism."

Loras was accompanied by his current secretary, Fr. Jean-Antoine-Marie Pelamourgues, who had come with him from France just the year before, and Scott Campbell, who also gave hospitality to the two men. As Bishop Loras wrote to his sister: "*The wife of our host, who had already received some religious instruction, was baptized and confirmed; she subsequently received the sacrament of matrimony, and made her first communion. The Catholics of St. Peter's amounted to one hundred and eighty-five, fifty-six of whom we baptized...*"

The reality was 185 Catholic "persons", then, and not "families", as the newspaper had claimed.

Mathias M. Hoffmann, in his history of the pioneer priests[29], further offers the names of those the Bishop recorded on his return to Dubuque. "*...Practically all the names were French, though two or three, like Quinn and Graham, were Gaelic...Jean Baptiste Latourelle, Olivier Rossico, Louis Brunelle, Amable Morin and the names of some of the women...Julie Ducharme, Genevieve Cardinal,

---

29 Hoffmann, Rev. Mathias M., *The Church Founders of the Northwest*, [Milwaukee, 1937] Mathias Hoffmann was a priest attached to Columbia, now Loras College.

Josephine Beaulieu, Isabel Madelaine...Marguerite Leclaire, daughter of Michel Leclaire and a Sioux woman, his wife; Françoise Marie Boucher, twenty-three years of age, daughter of N. Boucher and 'a Chippeway from Lake Superior'; and Angelique Martin, daughter of Louis Martin and Ouanino, a Sioux woman."

Williams, quite obviously, listed only those living on the opposite side of the Mississippi from the fort and the bishop recorded, apparently, those residing beneath it and at Mendota. Some may even have come to see the bishop from a wider area. There is no mention at all of Mendota's oldest settler [in 1820], Jean Baptiste Faribault or his family. In the year of the treaties, a Lt. E.K. Smith made a survey and map of the Reserve and reported to the new commander of Fort Snelling, Maj. Joseph Plympton, that: *"The white inhabitants in the vicinity of the fort, as near as I can ascertain, are: 82 in Baker's settlement, around old Camp Coldwater, and at Massie's landing. On the opposite side, 25 at the Fur Company's establishment, including Faribault and Le Clere's, 50. Making a total of 157 souls in no way connected with the military.*

This population possess and keep on the public lands, in the immediate neighborhood, nearly 200 horses and cattle. I am inclined to believe that this estimate will fall short of the actual number."

When Lucien Galtier arrived at his post in the spring of 1840, he received the impression that the place was virtually deserted. Let us allow him to describe his coming in his own words, written many years later at the request of Bishop Thomas Grace of St. Paul:

"On the 26th day of April, 1840, in the afternoon, a St. Louis steamboat, the first of the season, arrived at Dubuque, bound for St. Peter and Ft. Snelling.[30] Rt. Rev. Dr. Loras immediately came to me, and told me he desired to

---

30 The fort, the trading post across from it, and the Indian agency were all lumped into the designation "St. Peter's".

send me towards the upper waters of the Mississippi. There was no St. Paul at the time; there was, on the site of the present city, but a single log-house, occupied by a man named Phelan, and steamboats never stopped there."

The version of Bishop Loras was that the presence of the first steamer reminded him that he had promised to send a priest to the upper Mississippi and so he had at once put Galtier on that boat. It seems rather a strange business and one cannot help but wonder if there is a somewhat longer story behind it. A bishop should not have to be "reminded" by the advent of a transport to place one of his charges anywhere and Loras had already scouted out St. Peter's for himself with a view to possibly establishing a mission there. The opinion of this writer must be, on the evidence, that this so-called "spontaneity" was a cover for an impulsive act toward Lucien Galtier on the part of the bishop. Is it possible they had already quarreled or some sort of unpleasantness had passed between them with Galtier being banished from Dubuque on very short notice? Galtier's colleague, Jacques Causse, really did remind Loras, in an acrimonious letter, of how the prelate had once wanted to drive him from his house in the middle of the night at a time when he had been temporarily crippled by some means. What Lucien did not tell Bishop Grace he had mentioned to Loras in an aggrieved letter of his own in 1844:

"*I was dispatched in the evening, barely finishing my supper, to the mission.*" Father Galtier also wrote that he was none too pleased at the time, as his prelate had promised him fifteen days of rest after Easter and then abruptly changed his mind. While still at Dubuque, the priest had been performing all sorts of odd-jobs in addition to his clerical duties.

Galtier continues in the "official version": "*The boat landed at the foot of Fort Snelling, then garrisoned by a few companies of Regular soldiers under command of Major Plympton. The sight of the Fort, commanding from the* elevated promontory the two rivers, the Mississippi and the St. Peter, pleased me; but the discovery, which I soon made, that there were only a few houses on the St. Peter side, and but two on the side of the Fort, surrounded by a complete wilderness, and without any signs of fields under tillage, gave me to understand that my mission and life must henceforth be a career of privation, hard trials and suffering, and required of me patience, labor and resignation. I had before me a large territory under my charge, but few souls to watch over.

I introduced myself to Mr. Campbell, a Scotch gentleman,[31] the Indian Interpreter, to whom I was recommended by the bishop. At his house I received a kind welcome from his good wife, a charitable Catholic woman. For about a month I remained there as one of the family. But, although well treated by all the members of the house, I did not, while thus living, feel sufficiently free to discharge my pastoral duties; so I obtained a separate room for my own use, and made of it a kitchen, a parlor and a chapel. Out of some boards I formed a little altar, which was opened out in time of service, and during the balance of the day folded up and concealed by drapery. "

Galtier then named some names, thereby echoing the account of Bishop Loras: "*In that precarious and somewhat difficult condition, I continued for over a year. On the Fort Snelling side, I had under my care, besides some soldiers, six families, Resche, Papin, Quinn, Campbell, Bruce and Resicko [Rossico], and on the St. Peter side, besides some unmarried men in the employ of the [fur] company, five families, Faribault, Martin, Lord, and two Turpins. No event worth noticing occurred, except some threatening alarms given by the Chippewas to the Dakotas.*"

Perhaps that year was calm enough where the Indians were concerned but the "threatening alarms" did not cease and the result was what is known as the Battle of

---

31 Galtier wrote the English letter of introduction, himself. It is in his handwriting.

Kaposia, named after the village of Little Crow, the chief of the Dakota. The year was 1842 and a consequence was the death of a member of the François Gammel family, someone certainly not involved in the conflict. Gammel, a French Canadian, had a cabin not far from Pig's Eye Landing, his wife being a woman of the Dakota or Sioux. Father Galtier may have had nothing to say in his memoir about the tragedy of the murders of three persons living not far from him by the Chippewa, but this occurrence ought to have made him thoroughly sensible of the danger and unpredictability of the frontier once and for all.

On that day an Indian named Rattler and his wives came to help the Gammels hoe their corn. Two of Rattler's children were also present. The Chippewa shot one wife of Rattler and Mrs. Gammel in the field and cut off the head of Rattler's little son. The son of the Gammels, a small boy named David, and Rattler's daughter escaped harm, but the dying Mrs. Gammel was scalped while in her husband's arms. The other wife of Rattler was in the cabin due to feeling ill and Rattler was with her, unknown to the Chippewa, who did not think it advisable to enter a house they knew belonged to a white man.

It is obvious that these people were killed due to being Dakota. Rattler, having survived this incident, later died of alcoholism, and he had a sister named "Old Bets", who was quite a character of the area for years. After the Battle of Kaposia, she went around clubbing the heads of the dead and dying Chippewa warriors, exacting vengeance.

Father Augustin Ravoux had quite a lot to say about the battle in his own memoirs. He seemed to indicate that some white people may have been in danger, as well: *"Little Crow, the chief of the village, lost three of his sons, and a fourth one, being wounded, was in danger of death. He became enraged against the few families that lived at Pig's Eye, almost opposite Kaposia. He complained that they had given no information to the Sioux of the arrival of the*

Chippeway warriors, though they could have done it, and prevented the disaster he had suffered. It was, no doubt, an error, but exasperated by his misfortune, and being under such an impression, he gave orders to destroy all these families the following day, in the morning; so I was told. Whether it was a fact or a rumor only, all these families, except a half-breed family, fled away and came to the Mississippi Island situated two or three hundred yards from the St. Paul and Sioux City freight depot. The few families living then at St. Paul took also refuge in the same island. During the night Isaac Labisonniere went to Fort Snelling to ask prompt assistance in order to prevent the massacre of some fifteen families encamped on the island. Troops were sent down the river without delay. Order and confidence were re-established."[32]

Actually, the army arrived to stop the fighting but the soldiers of the fort were too late. The encounter between the two nations, those ancient enemies, was over in a couple of hours. The settlers may have felt safe on the island because, according to a witness of the battle, the Dakota at Kaposia had hardly any canoes and so could not reach them in a sufficiently threatening number.

LOCAL CHARACTERS

What Father Galtier may have meant was that he initially noticed, from the riverboat, only one actual house on that bank which later became "Downtown St. Paul", the very nucleus of the future city. The fort is a few miles to the

---

[32] In 1842 there was as yet no St. Paul and Sioux City Railroad and any freight of the area had to do with steamboats.

north of there and, certainly, there would have been no reason for steamers to stop at a nearly vacant spot—except for the Phelan place, which was quite a distance from any other habitations—in 1840. According to J. Fletcher Williams, "*Thus, at the close of 1839, there were nine cabins within the present limits of the city of St. Paul.*" It is not clear to the present writer what limits Williams had in mind, but there can be no question trouble was brewing for a number of the earliest pioneers in 1840. Some of those cabins would soon disappear and that is the reason there were not as many homes for Galtier to discover as there had been in the summer of 1839 when Loras was present.

There must have been some sellers of drink among the people near the military reserve and possibly some other vices, as well, because they had previously been driven away from it by the fort personnel. Once again, the decision was made, in the same year and season that Lucien Galtier arrived, to expel these settlers from their new squatter's camp near Fountain Cave, irrespective of virtue or the lack thereof. On the 6th of May those living around the cave were driven off by the army and every cabin destroyed. Regardless, the expelled soon re-established themselves as near as they could outside the actual boundaries of the reserve—as they had nowhere else to go with all their livestock. The settlers knew the fort commander, Plympton, didn't want them, but they also figured the proximity to the garrison afforded them some protection from the Indians, who would not likely attack them with soldiers so near. Despite the treaties and sale of land, the natives continued to resent what they viewed as the white encroachment.

In the words of a Protestant historian named Neil: "*The squatters then retreated to the nearest point below the military reserve, and there they became the inglorious founders of a hamlet, which was shortly graced with the small Roman Catholic chapel of St. Paul, the name of which is retained by the thrifty capital of Minnesota, which has* emerged from the groggeries of 'certain lewd fellows of the baser sort'"³³

So the historic move farther down the Mississippi was made and, as no subsequent expulsions were initiated, the die was cast as to the site of the future city. Fountain Cave, as it happened, was the site of a "groggery" of Pig's Eye Parrant, a character with whom we will become better acquainted shortly. But let us now pause to consider the situation of the young man, Galtier, at this time about twenty-eight and the very antithesis of Parrant in every way, excepting their shared French heritage.

It is written that Loras had Galtier on his way from Dubuque within an hour after he had been reminded of his promise to send a priest. How well-equipped, how well-prepared, can one become in sixty minutes? The answer is obvious and one envisions a man with only one or two satchels or parcels getting off that steamer. Certainly, Lucien had his breviary, the articles required to celebrate a mass³⁴ and perhaps an extra cassock and a change of undergarments—but what more? Hopefully, he brought with him a warm cloak. Mathias Loras had given him one-hundred dollars with which to begin the mission.

One can hardly blame the priest for wanting to quit Campbell's boisterous household after a month,³⁵ even though this was all in the way of accommodations that had been envisioned. Bishop Loras should have known from his own experience there that the arrangement would not have been satisfactory to all parties concerned for long! In

---

33 M. M. Hoffmann, *The Church Founders of the Northwest* [1937] pp. 129-130
34 Although Galtier later describes these being of very poor quality, a copper chalice losing its gilding and a paten only of silver without gold plating. He had to purchase his own altar cloth and only had vestments because he had brought them from France and refused to turn them over to the diocese when he came to America.
35 The Campbells already had seven children at the time.

retrospect, allowing Galtier to depart for St. Peter's under these conditions seems unconscionable. A man sent to a remote spot alone cannot simply be consigned to the mercy of strangers, especially on the spur of the moment with no prior notification.

Where was it that Father Galtier then acquired his next "room"? Was it a part of the Campbell house? Had he, by then, already gone to live in an out-building on the property of one Monsieur Jean Baptiste Faribault at Mendota?[36] It is not so clear, and also hard to believe that Faribault would have offered a French priest a dwelling such as Galtier described in a letter to Mathias Loras. Besides, it was noted that the Faribault gift had been "repaired"—evidently not well enough.

Galtier: *"God is my witness as to what I had to suffer there, and what was done there. There my life was literally a continuous succession of privations. There, during two years I occupied a lodging so terrible and so open to the cold, that Monseigneur [the bishop] himself in 1842, visiting the parish, at the mere exterior view of the house, could not refrain from exclaiming: 'Ha, I shall not remain here a long time...'* " Lucien's response was that the inside was even worse, especially during downpours.

By 1842, at least, there can be no doubt Father Galtier was residing at Mendota and not with the Campbells. It would appear that the building donated by Faribault was a log house which, being pressed into service as a chapel, became the first "church" of the area, preceding the one at St. Paul. It was in this same place that Fr. Augustin Ravoux met with what might have been a fatal accident. Ravoux spent a few months with Galtier at Mendota and claimed the following:

"During his absence I took care of the chapels of

---

36 Faribault, the fur trader, was considered a wealthy man by all his neighbors. In a single year, he dealt in 50 buffalo-robes, 39,080 muskrats, 2,050 pounds of deer skins, 125 pounds of beaver, 130 marten, 1,100 mink, 663 raccoons, 331 otter, 25 lynx, and 5 foxes.

Mendota and St. Paul...*A few words on the old chapel. Its dimensions were about 13 x 26 feet. The roof was heavy. It was covered with bark, and between the bark and the slabs, or boards, there was at least six inches of earth. In the corner of the building we had a small bedroom."*

In June or July the main beam of this roof began cracking while Ravoux was asleep, but the noise soon awoke him. The priest had difficulty opening the door to escape but, with a mighty effort on his part, it gave way and Ravoux was left standing in the pre-dawn dark, listening to the continued cracking. Immediately upon hearing of the incident, Galtier went to Chippewa Falls to procure lumber for a new building and so work on the first real church of the small parish of Mendota, naturally called St. Peter's, commenced on October 2, 1842.[37]

A Jesuit missionary of the same era, Father Augustus Thebaud, had this to say about the rough dwellings of America: *"The walls of a log cabin or of a frame dwelling need a great deal of attention to exclude the cold air in winter, and the rain in a heavy storm. But no attention whatever was paid to these requisites in Kentucky, and at Christmas-time, when huge pieces of hickory or dogwood were blazing in the chimney and you were seated in front, your face, hands, and shins were roasted, whilst behind a sharp breeze froze your very bones."* [38]

But how was a studious young man from southern France, fresh from the seminary, expected to have the knowledge to weather-proof his primitive home? Galtier proved to be a "handy" type, but surely he had never previously lived in a house of logs nor in such cold. If he did not already know how, lacking a servant, Galtier would still

---

37 The small log church was eventually replaced by one of stone, which still stands. The first structure was torn down in 1869, but the original wooden altar, a rough cupboard six feet long and three and a half feet high, is preserved in the church as an artifact.

38 Thebaud, Augustus, *Three Quarters of a Century (1807-1882)* pub. United States Catholic Historical Society [1904].

have been forced to learn to cook, wash, mend, tend his horse, paddle a canoe, and acquire provisions as best he could.

Returning to the expulsion of the settlers in 1840, Lucien Galtier, himself, commented upon it more than twenty years later:

"*A circumstance, rather sad in itself, commenced to better my situation, by procuring for me a new station and a variety in my scenes of labor. Some families, most of whom had left the Red River settlement, British America, on account of the flood and the loss of their crops, in the years 1837 and 1838, had located themselves all along the right bank of the Mississippi, opposite the Fort. Unfortunately some soldiers, now and then, crossed the river to the houses of these settlers, and returned intoxicated, sometimes remaining out a day or two, or more without reporting to their quarters. Consequently, a deputy-marshal from Prairie-du-Chien, was charged to remove the houses. He went to work, assisted by soldiers, and unroofed, one after another, the cottages, extending about five miles along the river. The settlers were forced to look for new homes; they located themselves about two miles below the cave.*[39] *Already a few parties had opened farms in this vicinity; added to these, the new accessions formed quite a little settlement. Among the occupants of this ground were Rondeau, who had purchased the only cultivated claim in the place of that of Phelan, Vital Guerin, Pierre Bottineau, Gervais and his brother, &c., &c. I deemed it my duty to visit occasionally those families, and set to work to choose a suitable spot for a church.*"

So it was now, down-river, that a congregation had

---

39 Fountain Cave—that is, two miles below the place they had settled after their first expulsion.

formed, needing the services of a priest. Some of it was comprised of men having newly arrived from Canada. In fact, it was two of these, Gervais and Guerin, who donated a part of their adjoining lands for the log church named after St. Paul.

As was previously mentioned, Father Galtier had occasion to be glad of the presence of Fort Snelling during his first year in the neighborhood. By the end of the summer of 1840, he had grown very ill. The itinerant priest had been visiting another location and came back to his home in a very bad state: *"... in the month of August, I returned sick from a visit I had made to a few families settled in the vicinity of Lake St. Croix. Prostrated by bilious fever and ague, at the military hospital, for nearly two months, I could not have recovered, were it not for the skill of Dr. Turner, and the continued and kind attentions of his good lady. My grateful heart will never forget the relief I experienced at their hands. Both the officers and soldiers also showed me great respect and affection, and twice, some time after, although they had their chaplain, I had occasion to preach and offer the Holy Sacrifice in the Fort. What most grieved me, while sick, was the thought that no fellow priest was nearer than three hundred miles to me; but most unexpectedly, God, in his mercy, sent me one, whose visit seemed to me as that of an angel. Rt. Rev. Dr. De Forbin Janson, ex-Bishop of Nancy, France, was then visiting the Northwest ; he arrived at the Fort, and hearing that I was sick, alighted immediately from the boat, received my confession, and spoke to me words of consolation and comfort..."*

The terms "bilious fever" and "ague" have not been part of the medical terminology for quite a long time but were very commonly used in the 18th and 19th Centuries. The first was a generic expression for any increase in internal body temperature where nausea, vomiting, and diarrhea were also present. It is difficult to say with certainty which organism had laid him low but the fact that he mentions "ague",[40] characterized by chills and fever or sweating, and was at the hospital for a full two months probably indicates typhoid fever, once known as "bilious fever". Typhoid fever was, indeed, a life-threatening illness with a duration as long as four weeks of very uncomfortable symptoms.

We may now imagine Father Galtier struggling up that steep path leading to Fort Snelling in his weakened state, wondering if he was fated to die in the wilderness within three months of having arrived. Had the garrison and the army surgeon not been there, he well may have, as he acknowledges. It would appear that, by this time, a Dr. George Turner had replaced Emerson and that Mrs. Turner was not averse to lending a hand with her husband's patients. One would think that few women would find nursing a fine-looking, cultured Frenchman an unbearable chore, his charming accent while attempting to make himself understood in English perhaps even a welcome diversion from the rather humdrum life at the outpost. And, of course, it was not likely the doctor's wife who had to empty Galtier's slops and risk catching Salmonella Typhi from his feces.

A traveler along the Mississippi, Joseph Le Conte, tells us a bit more about Dr. and Mrs. Turner: *"Our camping-trip therefore ended here. We sold out our tent and bedding, blankets and buffalo-robes, and leaving our trunks at St. Peter's under suitable charge, hired a boat to take us over the river. Having climbed the cliff, or escarpment, on which Fort Snelling is built, we delivered our letters from Dr. Holden to Dr. Turner, the surgeon of the fort. He received us with great cordiality, and invited us to stay at the fort until the steamer from below should arrive. We were given comfortable rooms in the parsonage, and invited to take our meals with Dr. Turner's family... We found Mrs. Turner a*

---

40 Derived from the Latin "acutus", meaning sharp or having "peaks". A "fievre aigue" in French was an acute fever.

charming woman and enjoyed her society the more as we had seen nothing but Indians and half-breeds since leaving Mackinac. We greatly enjoyed the dinner, too, for that very day the game-laws imposed by the officers themselves ended, and they had brought in about a hundred prairie chickens. Dr. Turner, a famous sportsman, was especially successful, his pack being about thirty."[41]

Once Galtier regained his strength, or nearly so, he resumed his duties. But it was soon November and the numbing cold set in once more with all attending difficulties.

Fort Snelling Hospital   Photo: Myra Jensen

Others had their problems, as well, including Pierre Parrant. Pig's Eye lost his claim near Fountain Cave on account of having defaulted on a promissory note held by a

---

41 *The Autobiography of Joseph Le Conte*, [New York, 1903]

man named Beaumette, the property and dwelling having served as collateral on a loan. But the enterprising Canadian found another tract of land and set up a shack in which he would live and continue his commerce in "ardent spirits". After about a year there, Pig's Eye moved to another location below Dayton's Bluff and, indeed, became so well-known that people really did refer to the spot as "Pig's Eye Landing" and mail was eventually addressed there.

Did Parrant ever attend Father Galtier's church? Probably—unless he elected to spend Christmas Eve alone, something few persons are wont to do. Galtier wrote a lovely description of one such "fête de Noël" but, before coming to the erection of the church, we ought to meet some more of the local characters and revisit some events of 1839.

Minnesota is a nice place to live now with central heating, snow plows, window-screens and air-conditioning but it was much less bearable when Lucien Galtier was there. He, himself wrote, *"The rain, the storms, the snow, the ice, have also given me much occasion of suffering"* but he failed to mention the hungry mosquitoes of the humid summers, hatching prolifically in a land of 10,000 lakes. Nowadays they are battled, but nothing could be done about them in the 1800s except to seek shelter from their bite. There were rattle-snakes around Fort Snelling and wolves added their howling to the eerie hooting of the owls after dark. Yet fireflies lit the night even as the stars, which, before big city pollution arrived, shone with a wonderful clarity.

There are few sounds more mournful then the cries of the lake birds of Minnesota, those loons. In summer, the sun could be shining at one moment and, in the very next, the sky could turn as dark as Egypt, signaling the advent of a tornado. Augustin Ravoux wrote of a twister striking St. Peter's in the summer of 1850, uprooting many trees. He also mentioned that the Mississippi was threatening the chapel, the water not having been so high in 26 years.

As a traveling priest, Galtier could easily be caught in

a thunder storm of a kind that can be terrifying in the flat Midwest with its descending streaks of lightning or a downpour. A season of heavy rains could render what was normally passable into a marsh of uncertain depth, into which the priest and his horse once fell, sinking in the soft mud. The priest survived, but he says nothing about the fate of the horse. Spring is a very welcome season in Minnesota and can be balmy and beautiful, but fall is spectacular with its fine, crisp, weather and trees displaying their gorgeous colors all around. During one such colorful season transpired the ugly business of the killing of John Hays.

THE MURDER MYSTERY

The reader will recall Lucien Galtier having mentioned seeing a house from the riverboat belonging to someone named Phelan. This building was down a mile or more from any other, but another man, called John Hays, had lived there with Edward Phelan, the two of them being partners in the claim business. Phelan had a bad reputation but, Hays, a former soldier, was considered a good enough sort. The latter had saved his discharge money, socked away at the house—or so the rumor went. In September of 1839, Hays disappeared under unhappy circumstances, but Galtier, of course, missed all the excitement surrounding the affair.

The Indian Agent, Maj. Taliaferro, made a record in his journal: "*Sunday, 15th September, 1839, a man, by name Hays, an Irishman, lost. Supposedly killed—even*

reported to have been murdered by the Chief Wa-kin-ya-ton-ka, [Big Thunder, Little Crow's father]. *No belief rests with me. I incline to the belief that his neighbor, Phelan, knows something. Hays lived with him, and had money."*
By September 27, Taliaferro wrote: *"Wabsheedah, or the Dancer, called at the office to say that his sons had found the body of Mr. Hays, lost some time ago, in the river near Carver's old cave."*

The spot where Hays met his fate was discovered by explorer, Captain Jonathan Carver, in the 18th Century. It is not to be confused with Fountain Cave. The Indians called Carver's Cave "Wakan-teebe" or "The Dwelling of the Great Spirit". The arch within was fifteen feet high and thirty in width. To someone like Carver, it seemed a strange place, and he described it as follows: *"The bottom of it consists of fine, clear sand. About twenty feet from the entrance begins a lake, the water of which is transparent, and extends to an unsearchable distance; for the darkness of the cave prevents all attempts to acquire a knowledge of it. I threw a small pebble toward the interior parts of it with my utmost strength; I could hear that it fell into the water, and, not withstanding that it was so small a size, it caused an astonishing and horrible noise, that reverberated through all those gloomy regions."*

Carver also mentioned that he noticed "Indian hieroglyphics" on the walls of this cave, so ancient as to be covered with moss, and that there was a burial ground nearby. The cave is situated under Dayton's Bluff, this last eventually becoming the name of a neighborhood of St. Paul. Captain Carver discovered the cave in 1766 and further described quite a magnificent scene upon leaving the place: *"I left the habitations of these hospitable Indians the latter end of April, 1767, was accompanied on my journey by nearly three hundred of them among whom were many chiefs, to the mouth of the River St. Pierre. At this season these bands annually go the 'Great Cave', before mentioned, to hold a grand council with all the other bands, wherein they settle their operations for the ensuing year. At the same time they carry with them their dead for interment, bound up in buffalo skins."*

    This time, a few decades short of a century later, a lone Indian, the Dancer, conducted the authorities to the site of Hays' remains, the head having been subjected to considerable trauma from blows. A warrant was issued by the Justice of the Peace, Henry H. Sibley, and Edward Phelan was arrested and interrogated. The suspect was then clapped into the guardhouse at the fort until the next steamboat arrived and, when it did, Phelan was transported to Prairie du Chien, because this was the seat of Crawford County, Wisconsin Territory, in which the crime had been committed.[42] Edward Phelan awaited trial, but few in the area of Fort Snelling doubted he was guilty. A certain Alphonse Gervais related that he had seen blood on Phelan's clothes and it turned out that blood-stained garments were found beneath the floor of the man's cabin when it was searched. Some people still believed the Indians had done the murder, but it was argued that Phelan had the greater motive, someone testifying that the accused had even spoken the words, "I'll soon get rid of him", meaning John Hays.

    About the time that Father Galtier landed in the spring of 1840, the trial of Phelan came up at Prairie du Chien. Some witnesses from St. Peter's traveled nearly 300 miles down the river to give their testimonies, but the jury couldn't be convinced of the guilt of Edward Phelan and he was set free.[43]

---

42 St. Paul was, indeed, included in the Wisconsin Territory at this time, being situated east of the Mississippi.
43 St. Paul historian, Thomas McClean Newson, claimed that an Indian named Do-wau or "the Singer" confessed to the killing of Hays at a later date. J. Fletcher Williams was of the opinion that this was the first murder committed by a white man in St. Paul.

SOME TRANSACTIONS

J. Fletcher Williams' version of the sale of Pierre Parrant's higher tract to Benjamin Gervais is too good not to repeat here: *"Ben. Gervais, on losing his home near the creek, in upper town, at once proceeded to Parrant's claim, before mentioned, and purchased of that swine-optical individual, all his right, title and interest to said real estate, together with the hereditaments and appurtenances and so on. Reader, what do you suppose Gervais paid to 'Old Pig's Eye' for this property, now in the heart of our city? Ten dollars! It is now worth several millions."*

When Edward Phelan arrived back at his own claim, he saw that a man named Vital Guerin had taken possession of it, no one perhaps figuring on Phelan's return. And, besides, half of it had been owned by the deceased John Hays. Now Guerin was apparently a claim-jumper since the entire property had defaulted to Phelan, who had been legally acquitted—or so Phelan thought. The latter, of course, insisted Guerin get off his land, but the Canadian managed to defeat the unpopular Edward Phelan by the means he described in his own words:

"Phelan called at my cabin, accompanied by James R. Clewett, as I could then talk no English. He demanded possession of the claim. I replied that I would not give it up, as I believed I was rightfully entitled to it. Some more talk ensued, and finding that I was not disposed to yield to him,

Phelan told Jim to say that if I was not off by a certain day—say a week from then—he would put me off by force. As Phelan was a large, powerful man, and I was small and light, he could have easily picked me up and carried me outside the claim lines. After making this threat, Phelan went away.

As I knew I could not deal with Phelan single-handed, I told some of my voyageur companions at Mendota how matters stood, and three or four of them, strong, husky fellows, came down to stay with me. A supply of liquor and some cards made time pass merrily. On the day Phelan had set to put me off the claim, sure enough, he made his appearance—axe in hand and sleeves rolled up—with Clewett as interpreter. Through the latter, Phelan inquired if I would leave. I replied, no. Phelan got very mad at this, and said, 'tell the damned little Frenchman I will take him under my arm and throw him off the claim.'

I then said to my men, who were inside, that I thought it was time for them to interfere. They came out, and throwing off their coats, told Phelan that if he did not go away and leave me alone, they would pitch him over the bluff! And, moreover, if he ever molested me, they would lynch him. Phelan knew they were not fellows whom it would do to trifle with, and, as he had just got out of one bad scrape, didn't want to get into any further trouble, if he could avoid it. He finally left, saying he would take the law of me. He thereupon commenced an action before Joseph R. Brown, Justice of the Peace, at Grey Cloud Island, to recover possession. Brown examined into the case, and found that Phelan was absent from his claim more than six months at one time. So he told Phelan that he had lost all title to it, and that I could not be ejected. I had no further trouble with him, and kept peaceable possession of the claim."

The finding of the judge against Edward Phelan seems hardly fair, as he had been acquitted of the crime for which he had been detained in jails for six months—whether he was actually the murderer of Hays or not. But such, apparently, was frontier justice.[44] Nor did Phelan's legal troubles end in 1840. Ten years later, the suspicious Phelan was indicted by the first Grand Jury to sit in Ramsey County on a charge of perjury. But Phelan managed to escape and headed for California. He may have joined a wagon train, some sort of caravan, but he never made it to his destination. The word was that Phelan behaved so brutally toward some other men in his company that they killed him, claiming self-defense.

Vital Guerin had been living a bachelor existence when he decided to marry Adele Perry, belonging to one of the original Red River families driven off the Reserve. Evidently he had had enough of the merry card parties with those voyageur friends of his and decided to settle down to the life of a diligent, placid farmer. The couple was wed on January 26, 1841, with Father Lucien Galtier officiating at Mendota. Mrs. Guerin's father, Abraham Perry [or Perret], had been so physically devastated by the natural disasters at the Red River and being deprived of his home twice on account of the expulsions at St. Peter's, that he never reclaimed his health and could no longer walk.

---

44 In those days possession was nine points of the Law.

A CHURCH IS BUILT

Lucien Galtier, in his brief memoir, relates how the site of the chapel was chosen: "Messrs. B. Gervais and Vital Guerin, two good, quiet farmers, owned the only ground that appeared likely to suit. They both consented to give sufficient land for a church, a garden, and a small grave-yard. I accepted the extreme eastern part of Mr. Vital's claim, and the extreme west of Mr. Gervais.
In the month of October, 1841, I had, on the above stated place, logs cut and prepared, and soon a poor log church, that would remind one of the stable of Bethlehem, was built. The nucleus of St. Paul was formed. On Nov. 1st, 1841, I blessed the new Basilica, smaller indeed than the Basilica of St. Paul, in Rome, but as well adapted as the latter for prayer and love to arise therein from pious hearts.
The church was thus dedicated to St. Paul, and I expressed a wish that the settlement should be known by no other name. I succeeded. I had, previously to this time, fixed my residence at St. Peter[45], and as the name of Paul is generally connected with that of Peter, and the gentiles being well represented in the new place in the persons of the Indians, I called it St. Paul. Thenceforth we could consider St. Paul our protector and as a model of apostolic life, could I have desired a better patron? With the great apostle I could repeat : 'When I am weak, then I am powerful,' a good motto, I am sure, even for an apostolic

---

45 Mendota.

bishop. The name, St. Paul, applied to a town or city, seemed appropriate. The monosyllable is short, sounds well, and is understood by all denominations of Christians. When Mr. Vital Guerin was married, I published the banns as being those of ' a resident of St. Paul.' A Mr. Jackson put up a store, and a grocery was opened at the foot of the Gervais claim. This soon brought steamboats to land there. Thence-forth the place was known as St. Paul Landing[46], and later on, as St. Paul."

    The location chosen by Galtier was the plot between what became Bench and Third streets and between Minnesota and Cedar streets. The names of the builders of the church should not be forgotten. Some probably recalled it as their finest hour. They are: Isaac Labisonniere, Joseph Labisonniere, the two Gervais, Pierre Bottineau, Charles Bottineau, François Morin, and Vital Guerin.

    At the time of his interview by Father Ambrose McNulty, Isaac Labisonniere [the same young person who had gone to the fort for help at the time of the Battle of Kaposia] was the last survivor of the above-named gentlemen and still living in St. Paul on Canada Street. Although nearly eighty years old, Labisonniere's memory of that time remained lucid: *"I remember well the circumstances attending the building of the log chapel in 1841. Perhaps by general consent rather than the appointment of Father Galtier, my father held the office of general superintendent of the building. Eight of us at first volunteered for the work; others offered themselves later. The ground selected for the site of the church was thinly covered with groves of red oak and white oak. Where the cathedral stands was then a tamarack swamp. The logs for the chapel were cut on the spot, and the tamarack swamp in the rear was made to contribute rafters and roof pieces.*

    We had poor building tools in those days, and our

---

46 Mr. Henry Jackson was the first postmaster of the area, his store also the post office.

work was not beautifully finished. The logs, rough and undressed, prepared merely by the ax, were made secure by wooden pins. The roof was made of steeply slanting bark-covered slabs, donated by a mill-owner of Stillwater. The slabs were carried to St. Paul by a steamboat, the captain accepting in payment a few days' service of one of the men. These slabs were landed at Jackson street, and were drawn up the hill by hand with ropes. The slabs were likewise put to good use in the construction of the floor and of the benches. The chapel, as I remember it, was about twenty-five feet long, eighteen feet wide, and ten feet high. It had a single window on each side and it faced the river. It was completed in a few days, and could not have represented an expenditure in labor value of more than $65." [47]

In the recollection of Augustin Ravoux, the ensuing winter of 1841-42 was a fierce one with much snow and intense cold, quite a trial for everyone living in the Minnesota Territory. In such winters of heavy, driven snows, an edifice only ten feet high can become more than half buried. The Dakota of Shakopee, having gone into the woods in order to hunt, were forced to give up on account of the depth of the snow and set up tepees near Monsieur Faribault's Mendota trading post for the next three months before returning to their village, which was at some considerable distance. This provided Father Ravoux with a chance to speak to them—and Lucien Galtier with the companionship of Ravoux.

Basile Gervais, the first white child born in St. Paul on September 4, 1839,[48] had missed being baptized by the

---

47 McNulty, Rev. Ambrose, *The Chapel of St. Paul and the Beginnings of the Catholic Church in Minnesota.*

48 According to Thomas M. Newson, there were no white girls born in St. Paul until "...Cleopatra Irvine, now the wife of Richard Gorman, Esq., born in...1844. Mrs. Gorman is a splendid looking woman and as good as she looks—a fine type of a beautiful Minnesota lady." The Irvine family lent its name to Irvine Park, a "high tone" area of St. Paul.

visiting Bishop Loras. His mother was one of the people who went down to Prairie du Chien to testify against Phelan and, just prior to the coming of Father Galtier, took little Basile with her so he could be christened. Not long after, his family moved to Little Canada, about ten miles from St. Paul.

Galtier, himself, reminisced about living at Mendota: *"The families which I have mentioned as being on the Fort side, at the time of my arrival there, had afterwards to leave; only two remained. I could not do much good, by continuing to reside there. The St. Peter Trading Post was the only ground left me. I removed thither, determined to remain steadfast as a rock. Mr. Faribault, the oldest pioneer of the place, a true gentleman, offered me a small house which I accepted; it was repaired, and I made of it my chapel, contented to reside in a small corner of it, until more favorable circumstances. I visited St. Paul regularly and occasionally St. Croix Settlement, then called Willow River, and now, if I am not mistaken, Hudson. In 1842, June 5th, Bishop Loras gave confirmation to a few persons."*[49]

During a short absence of mine, Father Ravoux, being at St. Peter, an accident threatened his life...Once more we had to make a mere room a temporary place for the Holy Sacrifice of the Mass.[50] *Hearing of the accident, I left St. Paul, went to St. Peter, and at once took means to go to Chippewa Falls, in order to get the lumber needed for a new building. On, my return, I put men to work, and on the 2d day of Oct., 1842, I blessed the first [real] church of St. Peter. From that time, up to the day of my removal, nothing deserving of notice happened, save the passage of the venerable Bishop of St. Boniface, Mgr. Provencher who for the first time, but not without much danger, went, via St. Paul and the U. S. to Canada, a new route hitherto*

---

49 This was the second visit of the bishop to the area.
50 Probably in Faribault's own house this time.

unknown. On the 29th of Oct., the little bell of St. Peter's chapel was blessed. On the 25th of May, 1844, 1 was leaving to better hands the yet barren field of my first mission, not without feeling deep regret not without leaving friends behind me."

Father Galtier's account of those four years is very economical. But we cannot omit the Christmas mass that he described so well in a letter to Bishop Mathias Loras, dated December 26, 1843:
"The Christmas Celebration and the end of the year have supplied me with the material for the present letter. As usual I celebrated midnight mass. A great crowd filled the church. Before the Holy Sacrifice began, all seats were taken, and it was with difficulty that one could make his way through the midst of the crowd. Officers, soldiers, Protestant gentlemen of the vicinity, and a great number of Catholic Canadians from St. Croix, Lake Pepin, St. Paul, and the Falls of St. Anthony were present at the ceremony. Some musicians had come from the Falls of the St. Croix, about 60 miles from St. Peter's, to add to the festive spirit of the celebration.
The sanctuary was lighted with a great number of candles, which lent a splendor of light altogether delightful; it was heightened by the draperies...and a garland of greens, in the form of a triumphal arch, which extended from the entrance of the sanctuary to the communion table. In the center hung a chandelier surmounted by twelve tapers representing the twelve apostles. In the front row on one side were the musicians with their instruments; on the other the children who were making their first communion, each holding a lighted candle and wearing a white material on their heads. Everyone paid good attention and derived much benefit. The singing began at half past eleven and did not stop. It ended with the Mass of thanksgiving, which Mr. Godfert had said. Immediately after the first

[communion], solemnly celebrated, he gave an excellent lesson. The number of communions was very satisfactory. I had three who came thirty miles in order to have the blessing of approaching the holy banquet. The feast was beautiful and made one forget the setbacks and sorrows, experienced elsewhere."

Particularly lovely is the expression regarding the candles, which loses something in translation: *"un grand nombre de cierges qui donnaient un éclat de lumière tout à fait ravissant..."*

Surely, among the songs, was this French carol, the chorus of which goes:

"*Il est ne, le divin Enfant,*
Jouez, hautbois, resonnez, musettes;
Il est ne, le divin Enfant;
Chantons tous son avenement!"

By late 1843 both of the chapels of the area were already too small for their congregations. According to an earlier letter of Galtier, dated December 12, there had been a new development at the garrison. *"The soldiers of the fort have been attending Mass regularly since the arrival of Colonel Wilson. His lady is Catholic and he, himself, views me with favor. I have had some soldiers sign up for the Temperance Society and I hope their example will influence several others."*

The priest's hopes for improvement of the drinking problem and a rash of New Year's resolutions regarding it were to be dashed within the coming month.

Monsignor Augustin Ravoux[51]

RAVOUX AND GODFERT

What a joyous occasion, indeed, for Father Galtier, people having come to his new church at Mendota from many miles around, an affirmation that he had not wasted his time near the fort, after all, his suffering not having been for nothing. Hopefully, he had led the singing for, according to Fr. Augustin Ravoux, Lucien had a splendid voice:

---
51 Minnesota Historical Society Collections.

"At Mendota we had a few half-breeds who were excellent singers. Father Galtier, their pastor since the spring of 1840, had taught them how to sing the praises of God. Father Galtier was a good singer. His voice was clear, sweet, noble, rich and strong. The half-breeds, his pupils, could sing well the French canticles, and their voices were no less harmonious when they were singing them in the Sioux language."[52]

Even the speaking voice of the young man was musical, his Midi-Pyrénées accent, which tends to be sing-song, probably sounded quite strange to the local French-Canadians.[53]

But there had been other letters to Bishop Loras from Galtier in a far less exultant vein. Christmas only happened once a year and so did Easter. In between, the realities of life still had to be faced.

Evidently, Lucien Galtier felt most happy and secure when there were other priests for company and, of course, to hear his confession. This wasn't always possible at these prairie posts, which tended to be lonely but, finally, Galtier had the satisfaction of knowing there were two others from the Dubuque diocese nearby. The first to arrive was Augustin Ravoux, who had journeyed from France with Galtier, and who was to take over the missionary aspect, that is go among the Indians while Galtier continued to serve the whites and *metis*. Fr. Ravoux had been at Prairie du Chien and, coming north in September of 1841, he began a remarkably successful missionary career. His proficiency with the difficult Sioux language is said to have been admirable, as well.

Ravoux seems to have had a constitution of iron and

---

52 Mgr. A. Ravoux, *Labors Among the Sioux or Dakota Indians from the Year 1841 to the Spring of 1844*, article appearing in the St. Paul Pioneer Press, Mar. 7, 1867 (?).

53 This southern French accent also emphasizes the vowels that others, like the Parisian, ignore. For example, the final "e" in "belle" would have been vocalized by Father Galtier.

was one of those low-maintenance people who can live in just about any circumstances. Even in winter, Fr. Augustin could curl up inside a buffalo hide next to an outdoor campfire while on a journey and not mind too much if his cover got singed by the flames. In advanced age, Ravoux recalled and related such annoyances, the trials of his youth, without mentioning the word "suffering" with regard to himself. Certainly, Ravoux must have suffered but, unlike Father Galtier, he did not have the dramatic sensibilities of a character in a Russian novel. The glass of Augustin Ravoux was always "half-full" while that of Galtier tended to appear "half-empty". Ravoux knew he did not cut a dashing figure and did not care. It bothered Galtier that his friend went about in ragged garb—probably a good deal more than it disturbed Ravoux, himself. The kind-hearted Lucien did not like to see his colleague looking demeaned, not realizing that eccentricity comes with its own protective shield.

Antoine Godfert, who had been ordained by Bishop Loras in 1842, arrived in Minnesota either in that year or the next in order to assist Ravoux. By the evidence of the correspondence, these two had a very rough time of it, so much so that Galtier was moved to intercede on their behalf. Godfert, himself, wrote the following to Loras:

"One side of our poor house is a complete ruin, open to the winds, where it rains as in the field and we find with great difficulty a nook to shelter ourselves in. Sometimes we are visited by a fox or by a violent storm. Mr. Ravoux has all the merit that a holy priest can desire in his ministry, but your Lordship must not ignore the fact that it has been suggested either by letter or by word, that it is of the greatest importance for the mission and for Mr. Ravoux—and I could add for your servant—to have a man who could look after our material wants, such as to accompany the priest, do the cooking, take care of the horse, cultivate the garden, and above all to make ourselves be feared and respected by the savages, all things that a priest cannot do owing to certain conventions that must be observed...'Man

of Great Spirit' lately said a savage, 'how is it that you work? Why have you not a Frenchman at your service?' and, without waiting for an answer, seeing the missionary busy, disdain him. Moreover, what a loss of time to enter into the details of cooking, as much mortified as we may be, all this time is lost for mission work."

The very green Father Antoine would have been far more mortified could he have envisioned the bishop's derisive reaction to such an amazing request. A servant, indeed! What were these young men thinking? What point was there in conforming to the odd notions of the savages when it was they who were supposed to be indoctrinated in Christian ways? If one could not afford to hire help, one simply did without it. Even an Indian could be made to understand that. Pah! Why not each missionary his own valet? In enlightened societies, men worked as well as women and the sooner the Indians learned that the better.

What was not mentioned [as Bishop Loras could do nothing about it, anyway] was another cause for the scorn of the Indians, that being the fact of the Black Robes avoiding intercourse with females, the rationale behind this being difficult to explain, much less understand. The natives might have been told that the priests were following the example of Christ, who was their God, but the Sioux were perplexed by such a self-denying God, who had once been a man. It made little sense to them—or why the fathers wore a skirt like a woman when the rest of the French were clad in breeches the same as other white men.

Godfert, after pointing out that the Indians didn't hesitate to ridicule the slightest mistake with the Sioux language—which even Ravoux knew imperfectly—turned to the subject of the horse which the two priests had been able to buy:

"When we asked for a horse it was not a fanciful thing, because without speaking of the many rivers we have to pass at ford, the marshes, the shifting sands, reeds with long leaves, and of the big and small obstacles we have to meet here and there, how many children and grown-up people we could have baptized since my arrival here had we a horse. Now, thanks to God and to the little purse I have received, I have bought one which will be used for visiting from time to time our dear Indians."

Godfert continues in a kind of eloquent wheedling: "What are 100 piastres[54] for a missionary, surely a trifle. They are soon spent; 20 piastres on one side for traveling expenses, 40 in another for a horse, here a rope, there some oats or various little things, etc. It is with money in our hands, full of generosity, that we can attract a nation plunged into the darkness of death. O Souls, bought by the price of God's blood what can I do? We need food and money for those starving Indians, and priests and brothers for their souls. Now, Monseigneur, Mr. Ravoux is asking for the corn you have spoken of to him, and the 50 piastres promised. The position of the savages on the Red River are quite different from that of our Sioux. The former have food, whereas the latter have scarcely any game or food at all."

The above missive was written to Loras on September 30, 1843—and was forwarded by the bishop to the Society for the Propagation of the Faith in Lyons, as such pleading letters sometimes were—in order to generate further donations. When, by November 8, no corn or money had arrived, Lucien Galtier took it upon himself to add his testimony to the distress of Ravoux and Godfert—the situation threatening to grow far worse with the coming of the usual fierce winter with its blanketing snows and sub-zero wind chills: "*It might happen that Mr. Godfert has shoes; but it is certain that his boots are badly torn and held together with some white string. He doesn't dare to borrow anything from me to buy any at the store. When one sees missioners reduced to such extremes, one does not fear to take up the pen in their behalf and to make plain*

---

54 *Piastre* was the French word for the United States Dollar. 1 dollar in 1843 had the same buying power as 29.13 current dollars.

their needs when they find them. How often have I not seen Mr. Ravoux with scandalous pantaloons,[55] and that principally because they have no one to repair the old clothes? They could do with an extra man, because couldn't they have saved time that way? Also, they should be better nourished. It's quite rare that they have any bread to eat; of this I am very certain.

Lately Mr. Godfert came to see me and said to me: 'While passing the Fever River I had a great joy, guess what it was? ' And then he told me: 'I thought that I would eat bread here.' Mr. Cretin is able to buy his bread and he very often receives little gifts which help him to live. I, myself, am able to buy it, but these gentlemen are not able and they receive nothing from anyone; they are neither one nor the other capable of cooking and they are scorned when they are found at the various details of the kitchen. The savages of this place are little understood by those who find themselves far away from here."

Galtier's letter to Loras, dated the 8th of November, 1843, reflects a discrepancy between the bishop's mathematics and his own when it came to Galtier's expenses versus his income. Lucien seems to admit to some sort of accounting error on his part but denies that he ever used any donations he may have received in a frivolous fashion, nor had he any debts. He tells Loras that he has enough funds to see him through the winter but rather crossly adds, "*I hope that I will never be asked to explain myself about my expenses as though I owe something.*" However, Galtier promises to keep an account of any gifts he

---

55 The priests often wore trousers under their cassocks, especially in winter. However, it may be that Galtier found it scandalous that Ravoux actually wore pants like a Protestant minister, had to, because his priestly garment was in such deplorable condition. In those times the uniform did not consist of black trousers and jacket but always a cassock or a robe with hood, in the case of the Franciscans. Later on, the Dakota women made Ravoux a cassock of deerskin, dyed black with the juice of berries, but in time the garment turned purple. Regardless, Ravoux continued to wear it.

might receive in the future *"so everybody will be satisfied"*.

The problems with Father Godfert seem to have manifested themselves quite early on, although Galtier, in writing to Bishop Loras, displayed restraint when referring to this young colleague and even optimism. On December 12, 1843, Lucien admitted Godfert seemed discouraged and was doing little studying of the language he needed for the mission. He opined the man *"will make mistakes if not overseen"* and offered to take Godfert under his wing, spend a lot of time with him. In his own letters to his superior, Father Antoine bleakly related that Ravoux actually didn't need anyone to assist him and *"was doing everything by himself"*. Perhaps what really discouraged Godfert was the knowledge that he could not measure up to Father Ravoux.

After the winter of 1842/1843 the ice was still on the Mississippi until the beginning of April and Augustin Ravoux was anxious to go to Dubuque to confer with Bishop Loras. The priest made up his mind to leave St. Peter's with the overland mail carrier, embarking upon a long and perilous journey. Impressed and perhaps even awed by the dauntless Ravoux, Loras handed him three-hundred dollars to spend as he saw fit. Some of it Ravoux must have used to print his religious booklet in the Sioux language, which the part-native Faribault family had helped him translate from French. Only paper and ink were needed as Father Joseph Cretin at Prairie du Chien had his own printing press. That is where Ravoux then headed immediately. This priest printed the copies with the aid of a lad of thirteen, who knew how to operate the press, while Father Cretin took advantage of the presence of Ravoux, leaving his church for a time in order to visit some isolated Catholic families.

Since, in the spring, Augustin Ravoux had been given $300. by his bishop, a great deal of money at the time, and Godfert should have arrived with funds, their extreme poverty of the next winter seems a bit odd. But Lucien seems to have been convinced of it and that is understandable with Ravoux in rags [pointed out by Lucien in a previous letter] and Godfert's boots falling apart. By now Father Galtier had begun to take a darker and even sarcastic tone with Bishop Loras, whom he obviously felt to be neglectful of the priests in his diocese. What was happening to those funds from France, anyway? Galtier probably was not given any explanations other than that Loras was having difficulty obtaining them. The bishop had sent an earlier letter, received from Galtier on behalf of Ravoux, to his chief benefactor, the Society For the Propagation of the Faith at Lyons. To this he added, *"My answer to such a letter was that the diocese could now offer nothing but a debt of 5,000 francs,[56] contracted principally to equip Mr. Godfert for the mission; that if the Catholic Work would still help us, the support would be used for the most part to continue the mission, and before abandoning it, I shall sell the chalice reserved for the offering of the Holy Sacrifice on feast days."*

So perhaps the "purse" mentioned by Godfert had, indeed, come from the diocese of Dubuque. In any event, he had once been given some portion of 5,000 francs. But just why this last constituted a "debt" is not obvious, as the annals of the Society show that Loras received 51,980 francs from it in 1841, 34,440 the next year and 26,600 francs in 1843. The cup, presumably, did not need to be sold because, before the 10th of November, Loras had received 14,000 francs from the Society. Hopefully, some of this money went for the relief of the missionary priests on the upper Mississippi, but what Ravoux and Godfert had done with the funds they had previously received is rather mysterious. It may well be they had been feeding those starving Indians.

There were various new settlers coming to the area, purchasing plots of land from those who came before. As it happened, the Indians caused their share of disturbance in

---

56 Appr. $1,000 US dollars at the time. After the Civil War, the gold Half Eagle of five dollars was worth 28.85 francs.

1843 and, in the words of J. Fletcher Williams, were "perpetually drunk". The widow of the Englishman, Richard Mortimer, who had died in the meantime, was busy packing up the unsuccessful general store her husband had opened when a native entered very quietly and spied a bottle of camphor on a shelf. Thinking it was whiskey, the Indian took a swig, much to his disgust. He then turned the spigot of a barrel of vinegar, hoping that it really was whiskey this time or something which might kill the taste of the camphor at very least. By this time Mrs. Mortimer had noticed him and ran for safety to the house of a newcomer, Mrs. Irvine. The enraged Indian, supposing himself poisoned, gave chase with his tomahawk but it was wrested from him by Mr. Irvine. Meanwhile, all the vinegar had run out of the barrel, causing the Mortimer establishment to reek something awful.

It seemed that in January of 1844, Galtier repeated to Loras his offer to mentor Antoine Godfert, the unspoken motive perhaps being to rescue him from his unhappy situation with Ravoux. Apparently Galtier viewed himself as a fitting role model and a more encouraging influence on the younger priest, but could not get the bishop to agree. Godfert remained with Ravoux. Therefore, in the same frigid month, Lucien Galtier foolishly [as he admitted to Loras] elected to visit the other clerics at a place called Petite Prairie, about 23 miles from Mendota—on foot and without snow-shoes. He was saved from certain peril by an individual who offered him a ride on a sled. Petite Prairie was located near two Indian villages close to what is now the town of Chaska in Carver County. There Galtier found Ravoux and Godfert living in their usual impecunious fashion in a house that probably belonged to a member of the Faribault family as it had established a trading post at the spot. The pair had little of anything for their private use in this chilly structure, even sharing a single coffee cup. It seems strange today—although no one may have thought anything amiss at the time—that Augustin Ravoux was also sharing his bed with *"the little boy who helps him as catechist,"*[57] due to the priest or the lad not having any blankets of his own. In the 19th Century, people were accustomed to two or more people in a bed. At least Galtier supplies this information to Loras in a completely nonchalant manner, being only concerned about the lack of efficient heating of the bedrooms in the dwelling.

Exactly who this child was is not specified but Ravoux, himself, wrote to the bishop at this same time and place, asking to be reimbursed for the money he had spent on clothing for the boy, who may have been an Indian, in addition to a number of other requests. In this very missive, Father Ravoux apologized for some of the expressions he used in a previous letter contra Godfert, saying *"they were perhaps a little too strong"*. Nevertheless, he added, *"I think that if the same things that happened should happen again, I would abandon the mission, if he were not recalled. Later details of the things that happened under our eyes can be given Your Excellency if need be."*

Although Ravoux had written some things rendered all the more damning by their lack of particulars, he claimed no animus toward Godfert. In fact, in the following March he suggested that he, Galtier, and Godfert might be allowed to visit some Sioux living on the Missouri River come summer. However, by the end of May the three priests had gone their separate ways.

Whose idea it was for Galtier to quit what was already the budding town of St. Paul is difficult to know. The parish was growing steadily and was likely to expand farther. Perhaps Loras had chosen to transfer him or Father Galtier really had burned out there after four years—we do not know all the reasons—but the one he cited to Loras was that same over-consumption of whiskey he had learned about in the very beginning.

---

57 A catechist is a religious instructor, so one would have to include this boy was not so very young if he was useful to Ravoux.

"A large number of soldiers have become members of the temperance society; but to offset that good, since a few days before Christmas, there have been saturnalian orgies, or drinking bouts, almost continuously, particularly on the St. Paul side. Tomorrow I expect to threaten them with God's anger, if they do not return to their duty. A priest is absolutely necessary at that place. Monseigneur can assure himself of that by the details already given. The Bishop of Milwaukee ought to be notified. I will undertake to write him...I am anxious to no longer have charge of these men...Otherwise I must always be among them, studying them, and altering them by the grace of God. But the work is hard—it would be easier to work a miracle and raise the dead than to convert drunkards. But one cannot always choose, and one must endure opposition." [from a letter dated January 6, 1844]

By now, St. Paul belonged to the diocese of Milwaukee and not Dubuque and what was happening there was, indeed, the concern of the Bishop of Milwaukee in the Wisconsin Territory. The Milwaukee diocese was not created by Pope Gregory XVI until November 28, 1843. When John Martin Henni went to Rome in the spring of 1844 to have the title of bishop conferred upon him, that is when the Milwaukee diocese was fully established. So, in January, things were still a bit uncertain. Eventually, St. Paul was designated the seat of a diocese of its own, but, at this time, it was rather confusing that Lucien Galtier served both the diocese of Dubuque and that of Milwaukee. At any rate, Bishop Henni was not urging Galtier to go, no more than he wished to replace his successor, Ravoux. Galtier wrote this assessment to Loras for the *Catholic Almanac* at the close of 1843: "St. Peter's, in Iowa,[58] with a chapel and a house for the priest, at the confluence of the river of the same name and the Mississippi, at 8 miles from St. Anthony Falls, served by Lucien Galtier. It has but 130 Catholics and

---

58 That is, being a part of the diocese of Dubuque.

these include the Catholic persons at Fort Snelling, and those of Lake Pepin which is 111 miles lower down than St. Peter on the banks of the Mississippi river, and who cannot be visited because of the great distance.

St. Paul, a new place and which increases every year, in Wisconsin,[59] 7 miles from St. Peter's, with a provisional chapel, is visited from St. Peter's. It embraces 454 Catholic souls (at least) and includes those at Little Crow, the falls and the entry of Ste. Croix, and the Catholics employed in the environs of the Chippewas River."

By the time Fr. Augustin Ravoux gave his own report in 1849, there were 650 Catholics in St. Paul and 150 at St. Peter. Lucien Galtier was still there at the turn of the new year, 1844, but some others, with whom we are familiar, had already left. Augustin Ravoux and Antoine Godfert had fallen out completely and Ravoux had left the northern missions—temporarily, it turned out. Pierre Parrant seems to have given up in 1843 when Louis Robert bought his claim, the one with the "grog shop". Parrant then made another claim next to that of Michel LeClaire. The two of them quarreled over boundaries and, out-litigated and ridiculed, Parrant took off in a fury for Lake Superior but died on the way. Despite an unsavory reputation, Pig's Eye did have his defenders. August Larpenteur, in a short memoir, recalled *"his word in a deal was as good as any other man's, whose word was good at all."*[60]

Others of Galtier's French-speaking flock sold their claims and went off, as well, literally in search of greener pastures some distance from the city that had started as—and would continue to be—such a colorful place. One of their destinations came to be called and still is known as Little Canada.

As he left *"not without regret and not without friends"* in May of 1844, and hindsight engenders nostalgia,

---

59 Meaning under the auspices of the diocese of Milwaukee.
60 Larpenteur, August L., *Recollections of the City and People of St. Paul 1843-1898*. Collections of the MHS, Volume 9.

Lucien Galtier made two visits to the spot he had enriched—as well as survived— in the years 1853 and 1865, by which time the city of St. Paul had expanded enormously. One has to wonder if, by then, Galtier did not wish he had been able to remain. If he had, perhaps he might have become bishop of the new diocese, created by the Pope in 1850,[61] instead of the worthy Cretin, who had never previously served in Minnesota at all.

Joseph Cretin offered this advice to his superior from the upper Mississippi on May 8, 1844: *"If M. Galtier experiences some difficulties and some uncertainty at Keokuk, he will prefer to return here where he had very little to do and where he found some advantages which very few of the other priests of the diocese have. He was able to acquire some savings and make some purchases each year. If he insists upon coming back here, I would urge Your Excellency not to go against his wish. He is rather sensitive and could easily become discouraged. He had made himself a little nest here and he seemed quite content; M. Ravoux would not be displeased if he returned, they would get along well together!"*

It is hardly likely that the "nest" of Galtier was as soft as Cretin described it, yet his remarks serve to indicate that the former was glad only to be relieved of the drunkards and not the rest of his flock. Cretin noted his contentment and also something else about Galtier, forewarning Loras to handle the young priest with care—or a valuable man might be lost. It was not like Joseph Cretin to advise his superior so obviously but this time he sensed that Mathias Loras had better not expect too much deference from a certain abbé. And so Lucien Galtier departed from the place with which he would always be associated and where he would achieve his greatest posthumous fame and honors. He wrote that his eyes teared up when the steamer moved away from the dock, but he never insisted upon coming back to Minnesota

---

61 Originally including Minnesota and the Dakotas, it was elevated to the archdiocese of St. Paul-Minneapolis in 1888.

as a parish priest.

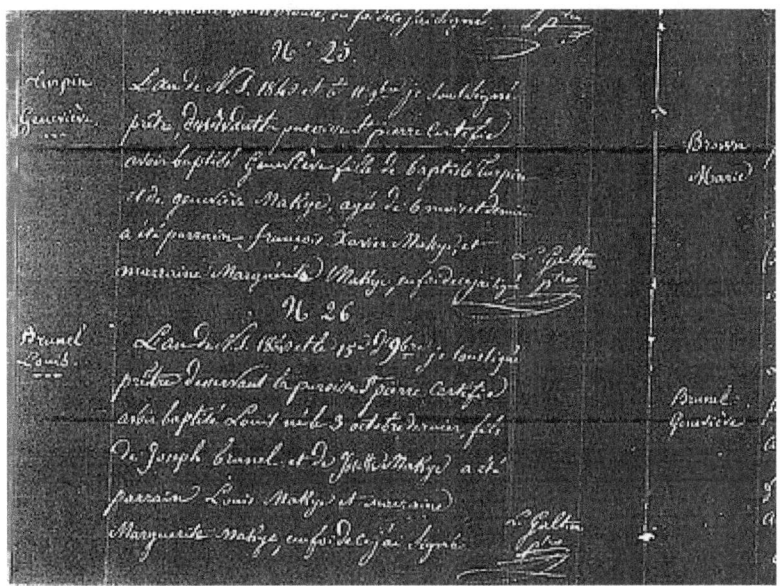

Baptisms of Genevieve Turpin and Louis Brunel by Galtier in 1840. Note the priest's signature, "L. Galtier".[62]

---

62 Photostatic image, Archdiocese of St. Paul-Minneapolis.

"A man living isolated from his kind grows weary from the apparent uselessness of his efforts. The intense heat exhausts his strength and checks his ardor. Too often he loses his life or in the fear of losing it he abandons his post. He is fortunate indeed if he does not prove the truth of those words of the Holy Ghost: 'Woe to him who is alone!' and from a being full of vigor and activity he becomes a good-for-nothing and the scorn of his fellowmen." Louis Dubourg, Bishop of New Orleans, 1826[63]

KEOKUK, IOWA

Father Galtier received his awaited transfer. Unhappily, for him, it was to Keokuk, Iowa—although, at this juncture, one suspects Lucien was so tired of the missionary life that no location in the diocese would have met with his approval. And he was not the only disgruntled among the abbés of the Minnesota Territory. Ravoux and Godfert had reached an impasse. Godfert was judged by Joseph Cretin, the arbitrator between him and Ravoux, not to have sufficient experience to remain among the Sioux. He was called back to Dubuque. Cretin had reported to Loras that the young man needed a bridle instead of spurs. By then, one might imagine, Antoine was not at all sorry to re-enter civilization and the prospect of his daily bread. However, it seems evident that Mathias Loras either did not trust Galtier to give him the assessment of what was transpiring between the two men—or he had already noted Galtier's reluctance to

---

63 *St. Louis Catholic Historical Review*, Vol. II, Nos. 2-3, p. 70. Louis-Guillaume-Valentin Dubourg, even though bishop of New Orleans with a see extending over a vast territory, nevertheless lived in St. Louis.

take sides.

A couple of years earlier, the sight of young Godfert traveling to an unknown fate had moved Augustus Thebaud to remark: *"The Bishop of Dubuque, next to the Bishop of St. Louis, has more Indians under his jurisdiction than any other Prelate in North America. An experience of several years has already convinced this zealous Prelate that we should expect to reap little fruit among them, if we confine ourselves to the posts where the Americans and Canadians pursue their trade.*

He has therefore formed the plan of directing missionaries to the center of the country, far from every village frequented by the Europeans; and during my sojourn at Dubuque, in the months of last August, I myself have seen set out the first of those who were to be sent. The Rev. Mr. Godfert quitted Dubuque to ascend the Mississippi toward its source, a few hours only after my arrival with Dr. Loras. It was an affecting sight for me to see a young priest abandon the society of civilized man, to risk himself alone in the midst of barbarians, who are still pagans, cruel by nature, and exasperated by the fear of seeing themselves driven from their country, as so many other tribes have already been."[64]

Thebaud was mistaken, however, in that Father Antoine would be alone among the natives where he was headed or that he would be far removed from a trading post. The Jesuit might have more accurately described the departure of Lucien Galtier from Dubuque, another young man who had no fellow priest waiting for him and who really did not know what might befall him at the hands of savages who had been slaughtering each other when Bishop Loras was among them.

Ravoux had also quit the Sioux country for a while, but returned to take the place of Galtier as pastor of the congregations at St. Paul and Mendota. He never left the

---
64 Thebaud, Augustus, S.J., in *Annals of the Faith*, Vol. VI, p. 879, written from Kentucky, October 15, 1843.

area again except to take an occasional trip.

Everybody was falling out with everybody else—but mostly with Mathias Loras. The relations between Father Samuel Mazzuchelli and Bishop Loras, heretofore good, became very strained when it looked as if the Dominican wished to leave the Dubuque diocese for the east. Another priest threated to sue the bishop for the price of his passage to America, which Loras had thought too extravagant and refused to pay. Jacques Causse,[65] a young man known to Galtier in France and who was one of the subdeacons recruited by Loras in 1838, became thoroughly disillusioned with his superior and sent him a searing letter, venting all of his grievances. Loras, deeply wounded, wrote Causse the following:

"My very dear Friend: Never have I received such a letter that has touched me more deeply than yours of the 8th. All the courage that I have, I take to tell you and the priests who have the opinion of me that you manifest, that you are obliged in conscience to write to the Pope so that he may place me under interdict; for your words imply that there is not in the Catholic Church a bishop more hypocritical, more greedy, more cruel and more sensual than

Yours very affectionately in J. C.
Mathias Loras "

Whether Father Causse actually wrote to the Pope is not known, but he became affiliated with the diocese of Milwaukee thereafter. Remigius Petiot, another of the original Dubuque missionaries, rebelled against Loras, as well, and threatened the bishop that, if he had to leave his post at Galena, Illinois, just because it had become a part of the new Chicago diocese, he would go back to France.

---

65 Both Causse and Petiot eventually did return to France. Source: *Memoir of Rev. Lucian Galtier : the first Catholic priest of Saint Paul* by Rev. John Ireland. So did Father Pelamourgues, after serving at Davenport in Iowa for 29 years.

Loras acquiesced and the man remained where he was, outside of his jurisdiction. Meanwhile, the bishop was still writing to anyone who might oblige for funds. In December of 1843, Loras had written to an unidentified friend, among other things, the rather ominous words: *"I am in very good health and busy completing an elegant church dedicated to Mary, whose statue will be placed on the pinnacle..."*

One of the things that Mathias Loras was criticized for—and he was judged by the lay people as well as his own missionaries—was that out of the thirteen churches built under his see[66], only four were actually capable of supporting a priest. Loras was also accused of being a speculator, of buying too much land for the diocese wherever a church was established. Of course, the real estate he purchased very much increased in value—although the bishop, himself, remained poor—but some said the monies for these purchases came at the expense of those priests in the missions, who lived under such destitute conditions. Before he died, Mathias Loras became the owner of real estate extending ten miles along the Mississippi River at Dubuque.[67]

The early history of Keokuk, a city in the extreme southeastern section of Iowa, named after a chief of the Sauk Nation, is not very different from that of St. Paul. It was a station of the American Fur Company, where the Des Moines River meets the Mississippi, doing its trade with the Indians, half-breeds and whites, mainly the French. Between what became Main and Blondeau streets, was a rambling structure called "Rat Row", otherwise known as the fur company headquarters. At one time only referred to as "The Point" at the foot of the Des Moines rapids, the later Keokuk also had its protective garrison, Fort Edwards, being located at the present-day Warsaw, Illinois.

---

66 At that time. There were more churches to follow.
67 According to Fr. Thebaud the Jesuit. However, that property would have gone to the diocese upon the death of Loras.

Henry Lewis, lithograph of Keokuk, 1848

Closer view of Rat Row on the levee[68]

---

68 Images courtesy of the Iowa Historical Society.

Chief Keokuk

"At the close of the Black Hawk war the Federal Government recognized Keokuk as the principal chief of the Sacs and Foxes. It is said that when the announcement of this recognition was made in open council, Black Hawk became so angry that he jerked off his loin cloth and slapped Keokuk in the face with it. A writer in one of the reports of the United States Bureau of Ethnology says: 'The act of creating Keokuk chief of the Sacs has always been regarded with ridicule by both the Sacs and the Foxes, for the reason that he was not of the ruling clan.'....Keokuk (the Watchful Fox) was born near Rock Island, Illinois, in 1788. It is said that his mother was a French half-breed. He was therefore not a chief by heredity, but arose to that position through his diplomacy." [69]

Legend has it that the naming of the settlement after Chief Keokuk took place in the saloon of John Gaines in 1834. Nine men were present and a decanter of whiskey was on the bar. Gaines instructed everyone who was in

---

[69] *Story of Lee County Iowa [Chicago, 1914]*

favor of the name "Keokuk" to step up and take a drink. The vote was eight to one.

Keokuk, as might be expected, had its share of local personalities, most notably Dr. Isaac Galland. Virginia Wilcox, making her home with her uncle in her youth, that same physician, wrote a very interesting history of the place under her married name of Ivins.[70] Her father, Major John R. Wilcox, was in charge of the forts on the east side of the river during the Black Hawk War, but Virginia was orphaned at a young age. She arrived in Keokuk in the same year Lucien Galtier came to St, Peter's, 1840. Virginia, being born in 1832 at Warsaw, was eight at the time. She seems to have married William Ivins in 1849 and was old enough to be a witness at a nobleman's wedding in 1844, [Father Galtier officiating] although even after that she describes herself as a "schoolgirl". And so she was for, if Virginia became the bride of Ivins at age sixteen or seventeen—that was nothing at all unusual in those days. The school she attended prior to her marriage was called Edgewood Seminary.

"I recollect a trip I made from Burlington to Warsaw[71] in the spring of 1848. I was just a school girl traveling alone. We left Burlington in a great lumbering coach at four o'clock in the morning, with nine passengers on the inside with four horses attached. The mud was hub deep; several times we were nearly mired down and the vehicle had to be pried out with rails. We did not reach Keokuk until nine o'clock that night, were driven at once to the wharf where a steamboat was just ready to start down the river. I asked the agent, Mr. Daniel Hine, to take me on board, paid a dollar for my passage and reached Warsaw at eleven o'clock that night more dead than alive, as I had been sick

---

70 Ivins, Virginia, *Pen Pictures of Early Western Days* [c 1905]
71 Warsaw is seven miles below Keokuk, but in Illinois. Why Virginia was going there, instead of to her home on the way, she does not say. Nor does she mention what business she had in Burlington. She may have gone to visit her legal guardian, who was not Dr. Galland, at Warsaw.

all day from the rolling of the coach."

At any rate, Miss Wilcox seems to have been no more than a precocious twelve years old when the new priest arrived in her town. He seems to have left a lasting impression. As it happens, Virginia Wilcox Ivins was the only person having seen Father Galtier in Keokuk who mentions him in writing. And even then she doesn't actually give his name. This is what she had to say about returning to Keokuk in 1842, after an absence of two years during which she had been attending school in Ohio:

"Many changes had taken place and the village was fast developing into a town. The Mackinaw boats[72] of the French and the canoe of the Indian had given place to elegant steamboats. A system of lighting had been established and boats could now have their cargo transferred around the rapids by loading it into barges which were towed up along the shore with horses, and reloading at Montrose, thus enabling more rapid transportation. Large quantities of freight were handled in this way, there being no other means of moving it except by wagons. Often steamboats would get fast[73] on the rapids and remain for many days and it was a dangerous task to get them loose from the rocks. Numerous houses had been built and the town was creeping up the hill. Roth, Main and Johnson streets had houses between First and Water streets, but as yet there were none up as far as Second. Lyman E. Johnston was then building the hewed log house on Johnson street which so mysteriously disappeared last year, soon moving into it with his family, his wife and daughter Sarah Marinda, who was my best friend...

The cabin of Louise Hood, the only daughter of Dr. Samuel Muir, was situated on Bank street near the corner of Second. Poor Louise had a checkered career. Dr. Muir

---

72 A flat bottomed scow, square at both ends, being propelled by poling and paddling.

73 Meaning "stuck".

and my father were warm friends and his daughter gave me her own history. Dr. Muir was a Scotchman, educated at the University of Edinburgh, who on coming to America obtained a position as surgeon in the United States Army, and was stationed at Fort Edwards during the Black Hawk war.[74] After coming west he married an Indian woman and had two children of whom he was devotedly fond, James and Louise. His resignation from the army was caused by an order from the War Department prohibiting the officers from retaining their Indian wives. Placing his daughter in the care of Mrs. Mark Aldrich at Warsaw, after providing for her maintenance and education, he took his son and went west to the Missouri river. I do not know that he ever returned to Keokuk. His daughter told me that they both died out west. Louise made her home with Mrs. Aldrich till she was grown becoming quite well educated and very much of a lady moving in the best circles of the place. At the age of sixteen she married Amos Van Ausdol coming to Keokuk to live. Eleven months after their marriage Van Ausdol died leaving his wife a posthumous child, and in most destitute circumstances. Being unable to support the child, she gave it to her husband's sister who afterwards disowned her on account of her Indian blood, and she was utterly friendless.

In desperation she [Louise] married Alex Hood who abused her terribly. She gave birth to an idiot child, and Hood was killed in a drunken brawl, leaving her worse off than before. In her loneliness and despair she fell a prey to evil. Augustus Gonzega, a half breed who lived at her house, became her friend and they were to have been married; but fate seemed to be against her for he was taken very ill and died without the ceremony being performed. She was the owner of two full shares of half-breed land, her brother being dead. This consisted of twenty-four town lots and an undivided share in one hundred and nineteen

---

74 Virginia's father was the commanding officer at Fort Edwards.

thousand acres of land, but no money or where to lay her head. The land sharks who were grabbing all the half-breed land they could get hold of, induced her to sell her shares for a mere song; and after a long life of toil and poverty she died in 1882, leaving her demented daughter a heritage to the county. She was our laundress for many years so I knew all about her. My uncle and aunt befriended her many times when she was in trouble."

The words of Virginia serve perfectly to set the scene for the entering of Father Galtier upon this raucous stage. We are now starting to get the picture, thanks to Mrs. Ivins, that Keokuk was no more genteel or peaceful a place than the previous post of Lucien Galtier. We will examine some of its other inhabitants, but first, Virginia remembers something about 1844:

"The pioneer church of the village was of course Roman Catholic. A lot had been given on the corner of Blondeau and Second streets, upon which to build a church; meantime a small house of two rooms was put up on the corner of the lot at the rear and here masses were said, one of the rooms being fitted up as a chapel, the priest living in the other. Weddings were also solemnized in the small chapel, one of which I attended, that of Elizabeth Hunt and Henry Louis,[75] my cousin and myself being the only witnesses. Elizabeth was a member of our family..."

Virginia's memory is a bit hazy here. No house was built. It was already there and belonged to the local sheriff, Morgan Anderson, who had put it up for sale.

"The lots surrounding the church were used as a cemetery. On one occasion twenty-five men were buried there who were killed by the explosion of the steamboat Mechanic in her endeavors to get off a large rock in the first chain of the rapids, from which circumstance it took the name of Mechanic rock. The priest was an elegant man, a

---

[75] Baron Henri de Louis, a Chevalier of Napoleon's army. Elizabeth Hunt was a granddaughter of Chief Keokuk, her relationship to the family of Virginia Wilcox being unknown to the present writer.

native Frenchman, most zealous in his work, preaching in both French and English, and was building the church with his own hands! I well remember seeing him at work on the roof in hot July days with his long coat[76] closely buttoned to the chin. My uncle and he were warm friends. He was a frequent visitor at our house and a most welcome guest."

VIRGINIA WILCOX AND DR. GALLAND

It seems probable that the Roman Catholic priest admired by young Virginia Wilcox was Father Lucien Galtier, once again about the business of building a church. At first look, Dr. Isaac Galland, Virginia's uncle, would appear a strange person for Galtier to have cultivated but, on balance, one can see why he may have liked him. According to Virginia, Galland was quite the linguist, having a knowledge of French, Hebrew, and the Sauk and Fox dialects.[77] But English sufficed with the priest because, by 1844, Father Galtier was proficient enough to be able to give sermons in that language. Dr. Galland was intelligent, articulate, and wealthy enough to entertain in style. If Galtier was a welcome guest in his home, that was a God-send to the priest during a troubled time. At Dr. Galland's one could get a decent meal, conversation, and perhaps even borrow a book However, it is quite apparent why the priest would not want to boast of his association with the physician to his superior. Galland was no Catholic and had even been a Mormon for a while. [78]

Isaac Galland was possibly *the* leading citizen of

---

76 Meaning his cassock.
77 Ivins, Virginia Wilcox, *Yesterdays. Reminiscences of Long Ago [Keokuk, Iowa, 1908], pp. 5-7.* Galland, aka "Garland", was not Jewish but may have acquired some Hebrew in divinity college as a youth.
78 In those days the LDS were looked upon as arch-heretics.

Keokuk. His niece wrote that: *"About the year 1837, the town of Keokuk was laid out a mile square by my uncle, Dr. Isaac Galland, who surveyed, platted and gave it its name. He was assisted in the work by a surveyor named Brattle, whom I remember quite well. Dr. Galland also named the streets, and squares, three in number...*

Dr. Galland had taken the plan of Philadelphia as a model, and our wide Main street was patterned after Broad street in that city. The Doctor had maps struck off...At the time of my first coming to Keokuk, June, 1840, there were a number of houses in course of erection, mostly of hewed logs with a few of frame. Daniel Hine had built a comfortable hewed log house on Water street between Main and Blondeau, bringing his family here from Warsaw. Madam St. Amant, one of the leading half breeds who could not speak a word of English, lived on Concert street between First and Second. Her son, Frank Labershier, [LaBuxiere] was the French and Indian interpreter. He was very handsome with much native polish of manner, a splendid specimen of a man. He died shortly after I came, leaving only his mother and two sisters.

At that time there were a number of French residents here, among them Maurice and Pierre Blondeau, Joshua Palean, Edward Brishnell and others, most of whom had Indian wives. Henry J. Campbell, whose wife was a Potawotamie half breed, had a cabin on First street between Johnson and Exchange; Alex. McBride, whose wife was a daughter of Madam St. Amant, lived on Bank street between First and second, and on the corner of Main and Water street, with a porch on the front and a garden back of it, on the slope of the hill lived Mrs. Gaines...Dr. Galland had built quite a pretentious house for the times on Water street between Main and Johnson street..."

Dr. Galland was born in 1791 in Pennsylvania while his parents were traveling from Virginia to Marietta, Ohio. He studied medicine in Illinois, some say, where he began to practice. But others report that he had no sheepskin qualifying him as a physician. The doctor had moved around quite a bit before coming to Keokuk. In his youth, he had been sent to William and Mary College to study theology, but left to search for gold in New Mexico. That not panning out, Isaac spent a year in a Santa Fe jail for unclear reasons. It is even claimed that, when the young man, still only 21 years of age, came to Illinois, he touted himself as a lawyer—not a doctor—but few were convinced of Isaac's legal expertise. He may have needed an attorney because he was accused of stealing a horse and counterfeiting. These charges resulted in Galland being driven out of the county on the Illinois side of the Mississippi river. But that didn't prevent him from coming back later in the capacity of a land agent. While he lived at Nauvoo, Illinois, Galland had been a Mormon Elder and the private secretary of Joseph Smith. But Isaac Galland became disillusioned with the Latter Day Saints or vice versa and he left the Mormon community, eventually severing all ties with that faith and abandoning three purported wives. Mormonism seems to have given way to Spiritualism where belief was concerned.[79]

Galland's shady past didn't seem to trouble him, nor did it, apparently, unsettle many others. Governor Thomas Ford made the following observations about Galland's political aspirations in Illinois: *"I had a good opportunity to know the early settlers of Hancock county. I had attended the circuit courts there as States-attorney, from 1830, when the county was first organized, up to the year 1834; and to my certain knowledge the early settlers, with some honorable exceptions, were, in popular language, hard cases. In the year 1834, one Dr. Galland was a candidate*

---

[79] The author has gleaned the derogatory information about Dr. Galland from a 1996 paper, "Isaac Galland: Both Sides of the River", by Susan Easton Black, Associate Dean of Doctrine at Brigham Young University. From it, one also gets the point that, while the Mormons felt themselves cheated by Galland, he felt the same way about them. The names of his Mormon wives are known, but the legality of the marriages problematic.

for the legislature, in a district composed of Hancock, Adams, and Pike counties. He resided in the county of Hancock, and as he had in the early part of his life been a notorious horse-thief and counterfeiter, belonging to the Massac gang, and was then no pretender to integrity, it was useless to deny the charge. In all his speeches he freely admitted the fact, but came near receiving a majority of votes in his own county of Hancock. I mention this to show the character of the people for integrity."[80]

Galland fared far better in Iowa, where he married his fourth[?] wife, Elizabeth Wilcox, the sister of the commander of Fort Edwards. In Keokuk, Galland was reputed to be a brilliant medical man—whether he actually held a diploma or not—but dabbled in other pursuits, as well, including real estate. His reputation on this side of the river was sterling. Dr. Galland was a patron of schools, began a newspaper, and was involved in just about everything pertaining to Keokuk.

This, then, was the companion of Lucien Galtier while he was engaged in the construction of his church, assisting the contractor, Hugh Guildea. Galtier had not come to America to do the work of a carpenter—but there was no help for it. Mr. Guildea could not accomplish everything by himself if the chapel was to be finished at some reasonable date. Either Lucien was a quick learner or he had done some building back in France, because he evidently knew how to do it all, down to the final plastering of the walls. The location chosen for the church was a commanding one. Situated on a bluff, it faced a view of the Mississippi as well as the perilous Des Moines River rapids. A Mr. T. Fanning, a Catholic gentleman, donated the timber. With the help of two French settlers and a boy, the builder and the priest cut the logs, hauled them to the river with oxen and further transported them on rafts to the construction site. The final result was a building 20 x 30 feet, 12 feet high, with a

---

80 Ford, Thomas, *A History of Illinois* [Chicago, 1854], p.406.

clapboard roof.

When Galtier first arrived in town, he stayed at the Hotel Rapids, run by William and Nancy Coleman, for a month. This was the same place where Baron Henri de Louis hosted his wedding celebration, spending all the money he had with him, according to Virginia. Meanwhile, for a rectory, Father Galtier resolved to buy the house of Sheriff Anderson. It would appear that Galtier also boarded at the home of Virginia's "Madam St. Amant"—or perhaps only ate there, for among his itemized expenses he lists "chez Me St. Amans, 11.00". [Galtier also refers to her as "Madame St. Amands"][81] The priest thought the diocese should actually purchase the widow's house, as it was more "solid" than the Anderson dwelling and put to Bishop Loras the plan of having the lady move into the Anderson house for the balance of her life, becoming the tenant of Galtier. Then her house would become the rectory and needed only an addition to become the church, as well. The plot next to the current home of Mrs. St. Amant struck Lucien as being a perfect spot for a future convent. These ideas of Galtier were imparted to Loras in May with the intention he would remain in Keokuk. He warned Loras against having any dealings with Mr. Hogan, who struck him as a bad egg, his assessment later being corroborated by Virginia Ivins. At any rate, the church was not built on Concert St., the address of Mrs. St. Amant, but on Second and Blondeau.

So on some days, there was the young niece of Dr. Galland, watching Galtier with rapt attention as he sat at her uncle's mahogany table or elsewhere in that beautifully furnished house. One wonders what she found so "elegant" about the poor priest, dressed in the same garment that he couldn't bring himself to unbutton in the heat of that summer—the only one he spent at Keokuk—hammering away on the church roof. According to Galtier, this cassock of his ["soutane" in French] was falling apart and he asked

---

81 Her first name was Marie-Louise but her surname is written variously. The lady's maiden name was Blondeau.

Bishop Loras for a new one before very long. Perhaps it was Galtier's looks or his manner that fascinated Virginia Wilcox, although she failed to describe him in the same laudatory terms as she did the dashing, ill-fated interpreter, Frank Labershier. Hopefully, Galtier had some kind words for the girl and didn't ignore her, as Miss Wilcox was at this time too young to qualify as one of those virginal "temptations" at whom it behooved one not to gaze. Galtier must have done something to make Virginia regard him benevolently even many years later, as she mentions him again in yet another book, *Yesterdays, Reminiscences of Long Ago:*

"He was a native Frenchman, a most devout man, very much beloved by his parishioners and greatly respected by all the community. After the church was completed, or at least within a very short time, he returned to France."[82]

It is truly amazing that a lady, surely not an expert on the Catholic clergy in the dioceses of the Midwest of the time, could not only recall Lucien Galtier so vividly but remembered that he went back to his homeland. Either Virginia asked Galtier's successor what had become of him or she had heard him say, personally, that he wished to go back to France—because that is exactly what he did. One tends to believe Virginia was privy to Galtier's plans because she was also soon to be gone. In June of 1845, the girl was sent by her guardian, a Mr. Marsh of Warsaw,[83] to St. Louis where she attended a boarding school for young ladies, not returning to Keokuk again until 1848. By then Lucien would no longer have been in Europe.

But, in 1845, one surmises, reading between the

---

82 [Keokuk, 1908] Here is an indication that Virginia refers to Galtier instead of his successor, Fr. Jean Villars. Villars, although from France, remained at Keokuk for a number of years and only added onto the existing chapel.

83 After being orphaned, Virginia was at first given over to the Marsh family who lived near Fort Edwards. Her parents may have succumbed to cholera, which killed a number of the soldiers of the fort.

lines, that perhaps Galtier left behind him a temporarily broken heart. It is rather obvious that Virginia, in retrospect, exaggerated his place in the affections of others in Keokuk as, in truth, Lucien Galtier was only in town from May of 1844 through perhaps February of 1845.[84] Or, he may have stayed until the spring thaw because traveling on the river, the main mode of transportation, was often impossible in the dead of winter. If the priest had found the degree of acceptance claimed by Virginia, it would have been a wonder that he would not have wanted to remain. In all likelihood, the handsome man was most beloved, from a respectful distance, by a preteen girl. However long Galtier's sojourn in Keokuk, it probably seemed all too brief to Virginia Wilcox.

    Other Roman Catholic clerics had visited Keokuk in the past, notably the indefatigable Fathers Samuel Mazzuchelli and John Allemann, the latter a giant of a man of whom it was said that "he carried his church in his saddlebags" due to traveling around so much. Both the Italian and the Alsatian were Dominicans. Just who had advised Bishop Loras that Keokuk was deserving of its own resident priest is not known, but Galtier soon came to feel that the plan was useless. "Paris is worth a mass" said Henry of Navarre when he gave up the Protestant religion in order to take the French throne at the end of the 16th Century, but Galtier did not believe Keokuk was worth his time. There were only half the number of Catholics at Keokuk than had lived near Fort Snelling when he first came there—and these appeared to be much less committed, besides. Of course, Father Galtier built them a chapel, anyway, as he had been instructed to do. It was given the name of St. John the Evangelist.

    In the summer of 1844 Father Galtier was in no

---

[84] Month of departure given on a document sent to the author by the Chancery Office of Dubuque. Galtier would probably have taken a steamer down to New Orleans and left for France from there.

mood to appreciate anything—friendships, admirers, a completed place of worship or the fact that there were at least a few people who may have needed him. He is very severe on Keokuk, although it was probably not too much worse than any other frontier town on the Mississippi. But now everything about it aggravated his discontent. Suddenly, at the age of thirty-two, the priest felt "old" and communicated this to Bishop Loras, also revealing a fear of what would happen to him if he became ill or disabled. He said, *"I feel my strength is leaving me"* but that may have been more psychological than physical. Even though overcome by a sense of hopelessness, Galtier was working quite feverishly, putting in such long hours that Hugh Guildea cautioned him to slow down.

"Since I have been in Keokuk I have worked almost constantly. I still have to make my own supper...sometimes having only coffee and bread or potatoes, he [Guildea] would tell me: you cannot stand, you are injuring your health...In Keokuk I then cleaned the house, dug a small cave, leveled the soil all around. I covered part of the back room, made a door, placed a small window, laid out a wood floor, and plastered a little. But an illness stopped me. I went 4 times to the country, and once to supervise work in the woods. I felt very tired. I had to sleep in the house of a widow, not being able to get into a canoe. I felt very sick."

This is from a letter to the prelate, dated November 8, 1844. Simultaneously, Galtier rendered a description of the different kinds of carpentry he had accomplished and it is very impressive, indeed. But keeping occupied did nothing for his emotional state. *"Truly, there is nobody sadder than a priest who is sad,"* wrote Galtier, wondering what there would be left for him in this town when all the mind-numbing labor was finally done. *"I don't want to be all the time a plasterer, a carpenter, a cook, and others, but only a priest, a holy priest, and a priest a little more involved than in Keokuk."*

Lucien Galtier did not need to tell the bishop

[although he did] that, in France, a parish priest had someone to make his meals and wash and mend his linen. Even Jesus, he reminded Loras, had some holy women who cared for him. But he, Galtier, could now not even make himself presentable, having no decent clothing. His only cassock was worn out and dirty. It probably did not smell very good as the priest mentioned "sweat" in nearly every letter from Keokuk. *"I was, then, destined to water with my sweat an uncultivated and ungrateful field where the thorns and brambles suffocate the little good grain that providence placed there."*[85]

He had no articles with which to celebrate a mass when he arrived, having left the ones he had in Minnesota. In his opinion, he was inadequate in confession, evidently not knowing the right English terms for the varieties of sin and could not properly counsel the penitents. This had never been the case in Minnesota, where French was the reigning tongue. He felt unwell and had no one to tend him, evidently now living by himself in the Anderson place *"...without [even] a child, in case of illness, to warm some water."* One evening, having nothing to eat, Galtier went out to beg for a cup of tea that *"was my supper and my medicine"*. By December it seemed he was no longer visiting Dr. Galland [or perhaps Galland was not available that day] because he mentioned going to see a physician due to a fever and throbbing headache and not being given so much as a glass of water by the healer. But it happened that a Catholic came along and, when asked for help, called another doctor for Galtier. For a mere hamlet, Keokuk was not lacking in physicians. Virginia Ivins: *"The medical profession was also well represented by skillful practitioners, earliest among them being Dr. Isaac Galland, Dr. F. M. Collins, Drs. Hover and Hains, and a few years later Dr. John F. Sanford who first established the Keokuk Medical College in 1849..."*

---

85 To Loras, October 12, 1844.

"*I really see no advantage,*" Galtier finally wrote to Loras, "*of remaining in this post, which according to all standards, temporal and spiritual, is perhaps the very lowest in America.*" and "*I am giving you the report of my parish. I do not know what the number of inhabitants is in Keokuk. That of the Catholics is seventy-four, large and small. I have baptized six children, one of which was later buried by a minister. I have blessed two marriages and rehabilitated a third. One person made his First Communion and fourteen persons received Communion. One Christian was converted to the Catholic religion, two boys are taking catechism. I have no Catholic school. The revenue of the church is nothing. I have received some small offerings of victuals. I have been obliged to do all the furnishing of the church. The church is naked and without benches. It will soon be a widow and without a priest like other places of little importance. For the good of the parish a neighboring priest should visit it from time to time.[86] I do not see any good that can be done. I do not visit any other places, although twice I have journeyed in Missouri taking care of the sick, and twice I have been at West Point and Fort Madison...If a refusal for my exeat comes with your response, which I hope will be accelerated, I shall write to France the necessary comment to my disappointment.*"

Mathias Loras clearly wanted Lucien to spend his own savings on his upkeep and articles for the new chapel, but the priest refused to turn himself into a complete pauper without options and made it plain to his superior that he expected the minimum salary that the synod had guaranteed each missionary. Galtier did not hesitate to say that his own money was intended for returning to France.[87]

Although the Catholic population of Keokuk does seem very slight in terms of the ability to keep a priest, that could change with time—but Father Galtier did not believe in the possibility. For him it was a dead town, especially in the

---

86 As had been done in the past.
87 The passage cost about 1,000 francs or 200 US dollars.

time of "high water". Not knowing the main reason behind Galtier's animus toward Keokuk and its residents, we can make the educated guess that he mostly wished to be quits with the tight-fisted Loras and the anticipation of his lack of adequate support. Things being as they were in Keokuk, the priest would have no choice but to be dependent upon his bishop. Although by August the bishop had sent him nearly $600 for the church project, after that month the record of the contributions of Loras falls off, leading interested commentators on the history of the parish to believe that Lucien Galtier must have departed Keokuk in August of 1844.

But there is the letter, dated January 13, 1845, wherein Galtier writes, "*I am giving you the report of my parish...*", a positive indication he was still there. Moreover, there is a letter among the correspondence of Mathias Loras, bearing no name and address, but perhaps a copy of one that had been sent. In it he exhorts someone to fill in an attached check and give him a complete report of a parish with a deadline of between January 1 and 15 of 1845. The bishop says, "*The extent of your mission will, in my opinion, be determined exactly by that time.*" The fact that Loras temporarily defines the northern border of the mission as being the town of Cascade and the southern West Point [quite a distance] indicates eastern Iowa and that the recipient, or intended recipient, could have been Father Galtier.[88]

---

[88] Or it can have been Fr. John Allemann, residing at Fort Madison about 23 miles north of Keokuk.

GALTIER WANTS OUT

But it is certain that, by now, Galtier was no longer interested in the extent of the mission and the details of his own January letter to his superior are given very tersely. He might have become that kind of priest so pessimistically described by Bishop Dubourg, drained of energy and  patience. Dubourg, [at left] who for a while had the distinction of being the handsomest prelate in North America, himself lost patience with this continent, and departed to become an archbishop in France. Dubourg, who was reputed to be able to speak Latin as well as Cicero, died in 1833, five years before Galtier arrived in New York.

Asking for an *exeat* is something different from requesting a transfer. It effectively meant that Father Galtier no longer wished to be a part of the diocese of Dubuque. *"O missions of Iowa, how you are scabrous and sterile! O generous priests of Iowa, what you must suffer!"*[89] Also, simply, *"I am sick of the missions..."*

Now the Keokuk of the time may have seemed like Hell's Front Porch to a burnt out abbé and yet, in the memoirs of Virginia Ivins, it is represented as being a rather fun place. The difference all boiled down to a state of mind —and personal freedom. One party was a lively, observant

---

89 Quotation from a letter of Galtier to Loras.

child and young woman to whom life was an adventure and the other was a man, albeit still young, who'd had it up to his white collar with adventure and the trials it routinely brought him. Not only that but Lucien Galtier, at this juncture, had had a chance to learn that being a priest was not exactly what it had seemed in France. No longer a starry-eyed seminarian, he had found out that, in addition to the impoverished lifestyle, the existence of a parish priest could be quite lonely and the evenings, especially, very long. Perhaps Galtier had begun to comprehend why some priests took to abusing alcohol and others—God forbid—even became entangled in love affairs. *"Woe to him who is alone!"*, indeed. Galtier hadn't seen a grand cathedral or a truly beautiful house of worship in years. In his part of America, even God seemed reduced to the state of a pauper, ignored by people in a way that the priest had not known in his French youth. Nobody seemed to fear His wrath in Keokuk, that den of scoundrels, adventurers, and brazen females. Had Lucien been in a better frame of mind, less despondent, less judgmental, he might have been challenged by and enjoyed rowdy Keokuk much more—in the way that Virginia Wilcox did:

"Mrs. Gaines...was a well known character; she was a New Engand woman whose father on coming west to St. Louis had married a French woman for his second wife, his daughter thus becoming familiar with French customs. She came to Keokuk as the reputed wife of John Gaines, who died shortly after, leaving her alone among strangers quite penniless with two small boys by her former marriage. She was obliged to do something to support herself and them. When her strenuous life began she donned turban and handkerchief in imitation of French women and went to cooking, keeping boarders and managing the affairs of the town to such an extent that she was dubbed the Mayor. She became coarse and hard, losing the fair, delicate looks of her youth, took to swearing in both French and English boasting she would shoot any one who molested her, and I

think she would ; at any rate I saw her chase a man a block with an old pistol which had neither lock or barrel. The men were all afraid of her, or pretended to be, and she assumed the position of arbitrator in many of the disagreements and disputes naturally arising in such a varied population. "
    Mrs. Gaines may have lost her looks, but Virgina also wrote that there "*were many very pretty girls, some of them beautiful*" in Keokuk, a situation that might have motivated many a young bachelor—but not a priest—to remain there. Nowadays, a small-town clergyman like Galtier could attend the community dances and sleighing parties without penalty, but that was unthinkable in 1844. Neither, of course, was there television, a movie theater, or even a radio on which a priest could listen to some good music or a ballgame. There was nothing to do but work, walk, or read the Bible, a shortage of interesting or acceptable books being expected in this environment.
    The exercise that Mathias Loras had in mind for Father Galtier was building a fence around the 12 lots purchased as church property, again with his own hands. On December 26 the priest wrote to the bishop that he was not about to do this manual labor for less than 250 dollars and the job would have to be done before the first of April, his intended date of departure from Keokuk.[90] Galtier also told Loras that he had received $45. "*which took so long on the way that another $45.00 should have accompanied it, but for this, I am waiting till spring. I know from experience that one needs to persevere in one's requests.*" Probably, Lucien knew he would not have to put up that fence as there was little chance of him getting $250. out of the prelate of Iowa.
    In the Milwaukee diocese in about the same time frame, there was a priest named Otto Skolla, who attempted to alleviate his solitude by talking to his cat in the way that cat-fanciers do and playing chess against himself. In order

---

90 Loras made a notation on the letter that he thought there should be a fence post every sixteen feet, holes presumably to be dug by Galtier.

to better assess his positions, Skolla used to move from one side of a table to the other, sometimes quite swiftly. The Menominee Indians of his mission were given to spying through the cracks in his cabin walls in order to ascertain what a Black Robe actually did when he was alone. This business of addressing a feline and running around a table convinced the Indians that the priest must be the servant of a demon at most or crazy or drunk, at least![91]

But the low condition of the town that Father Galtier described to his bishop was also corroborated by Virginia: *"As a natural consequence, owing to the unsettled state of affairs, rowdyism and dishonesty were rampant and Keokuk bore an unenviable reputation. As an excuse for their evil doings a vigilance committee was organized among the frequenters of the small saloons which had sprung up on the levee, headed by one Dr. Hogan, a protege of Mrs. Gaines, with the avowed object of protecting the citizens but in reality for quite the reverse. No one's affairs was exempt from their interference and an almost unbearable state of things existed. On one occasion the clothesline of L. B. Fleak had been robbed of the week's washing. The vigilants went to work ostensibly to ferret out the offender. Several different parties were accused of the theft but proved their innocence. At this juncture a man from some where up the country came to town on his way to St. Louis. He was at once pointed out as the criminal and notified to leave town before sundown or be lynched that night."*

Yet there was always Dr. Isaac Galland to be reckoned with. All historians may not agree that he was a pioneering paragon—but the pen of his niece shows that the

---

[91] Father Skolla was at Keshena in northern Wisconsin where the Menominee had been re-settled from Lake Poygan due to a cholera epidemic there on account of bad water. Florimond Bonduel and Rosalie Dousman had also taught at Keshena, but Bonduel left due to difficulties with the Indian Agent and also Oshkosh, chief of the Menominee. Mrs. Dousman and/or her daughters continued the school until 1870, when it was closed.

physician certainly had honorable qualities. He took that accused stranger, whom he felt to be completely innocent, into his house. When thirty or forty vigilantes came to take the man away "*or tear the house down*", Dr. Galland faced them alone on the front steps, armed with a revolver and a huge bowie knife, which he flashed in the moonlight. The sight of the weapons and the sound of the doctor's proverbial strong command of the English language discouraged the mob, which dispersed.

Defending the underdog seems to have been a habit of the fiery Galland:

"There was resident in town just one negro named John who had been a slave belonging to a wealthy farmer in Missouri by the name of Mitchell. John was a most reliable negro. He had bought his freedom from his former master and had about six hundred dollars laid by in his trunk with which to buy his wife. The vigilants at once turned their attention to John as he seemed easy prey, accusing him of the theft and ordering him to leave town; his trunk was searched and his money taken and the poor negro was in terrible straits. One evening my uncle walked down to the levee, not knowing of the trouble till he reached the scene, where he found Dr. Hogan horsewhipping John with the crowd looking on, not one lifting a hand to protect him. My uncle always carried a stout cane and he immediately stepped up to Hogan and began laying it on most vigorously, ordering him to let the poor negro alone.

No one came to the rescue of the ruffian and he for once in his life received a merited punishment. After giving him a severe chastisement Dr. Galland talked long and earnestly to the men, telling them what a bad reputation the place was having abroad from such outrages, and appealing to their better nature to redeem themselves and help build up a town in which it would be a pride and pleasure to live. That he wished to live amicably with his neighbors, but did not intend to stand by and witness any more such outrages, that there were other means to deal with offenders besides lynching, but if it was to be a constant fight he proposed to take a hand. There was no more lynching, but threats of vengeance against Dr. Galland were like mutterings of distant thunder that did not materialize. Poor John, however, left town the next day carrying an empty trunk."

One may surmise that, as long as Galland was on his side, Father Galtier would have a champion in Keokuk. But the doctor could not help him with his inner struggles. Galtier was having his battle with his own superior and his weapon was his pen, sharpened by a masterful usage of his native tongue. While demanding his release, he couldn't resist reminding Bishop Loras of what he had faced at St. Peter's and what he had accomplished despite it: *"All of St. Pierre and St. Paul and the Fort are able to serve in testimony of my privations. Three times I ran the very imminent danger of losing my life...The rain, the storms, the snow, the ice, have also given me much occasion of suffering. Meanwhile, two churches were built; they are not rich as masterpieces of architecture, but they attest the sentiments of a poor priest..."*

Galtier then made a statement that summed up his feelings about the integrity of the bishop: *"The murmurs out loud on the failure of your word of honor, Monseigneur, are in sufficiently large number. Dubuque, Holy Cross, Allcamp, can be cited, and the persons interested are able to give satisfaction better than I. One priest from Dubuque said to me: Monseigneur, the Bishop, is so well known now that no one is willing to be held by his word."*

In a subsequent letter, Galtier proves not very apologetic but even cynical: *"I am very sensible of the pain which my letter caused you, and I am still more surprised that my statements have been the occasion of your tears. That was neither the object of my letter nor the intention I had when writing it."*

Having been advised, then, in no uncertain terms of how much the young priest desired to leave the Iowa missions, Mathias Loras still asked him for patience and endurance, so as not to scandalize and discourage the other clerics. But Father Galtier had endured enough for the moment. His response was heated and contemptuous: "*Does Monseigneur know the reason which caused me to come to America? It was almost envy of seeing the ecclesiastics in the seminary at Rodez departing for the foreign missions, and an association formed itself under the auspices of the venerable Monseigneur Flaget.*[92] *It was necessary to give a good example. I offered myself and I fortified Mr. Causse in the same work. My director said to me: 'Go, after 4 or 5 years you can return if the missions do not please you, at least the start will have been given.'*

Indeed, it was given and several of my friends were directed to different parts of the world, Dubuque seeming to be a place which was not able to attract them as other states of the Union. My brother, already a director for many years at the seminary at Toulouse, spoke to me in the same language. My father wept with great tears for some time before my departure and for all consolation wrote me a note that he hoped to see me again some day. All these gentlemen did not suppose that quitting the mission was to give scandal and discouragement to others...

As to the rest, am I scandalized because Mr. Mazzuchelli remains always in Illinois; because Mr. Petiot refuses to serve in the diocese and remains in Galena, because Mr. Causse is far more pleased to be at Potosi than in Dubuque; that Mr. Allemann is quitting, for motives that I do not know?"

Galtier is, by this last, reminding Bishop Loras that he has remained loyal to him longer than some others, although he was mistaken about the exit of Father Allemann, who served in Iowa for several more years. And

---

92 Bishop Benedict Joseph Flaget headed the Bardstown diocese in Kentucky until 1841 and then held the episcopal seat at Louisville when the see was transferred in that year. Apparently, Bishop Flaget made some trips to the French seminaries to recruit missionaries for America.

how has he been repaid for that fidelity? With corrupt Keokuk and its seventy-four indifferent Catholics!

The letter written by Father Galtier to his superior on the day after Christmas, 1844, is nothing at all like the jubilant one he had penned on the same day the year before. In fact, it does not even mention a Christmas celebration of any kind. Evidently, due to some previous complaints, Loras had written the warning: *"...never let people know that you are a victim doomed to death; it is quite outrageous for your superiors and very wrong."*[93] Exactly what the bishop meant is not terribly clear, but he seems to have cautioned Galtier to hide his depression, and not to let on that Loras, himself, might have been the cause of it.

Father Galtier stated this caveat was not even worthy of commentary. He had not characterized himself as a victim "dévouée a la mort", nor was he playing the martyr. The priest wryly commented, *"I am not shown at least from the outside as an enemy of the cross."* Anyway, he could not visit Fort Madison due to not having a horse and, since most of the Catholics there knew only German, could not make himself understood. If those people had refused to give support to Father John Allemann, who did speak German, how could he, Galtier, be expected to fare better in getting money out of them? On the last occasion of his journey to that mission, Galtier could not even recoup the dollar spent to pay his way up river. Allemann, himself, was avoiding stingy Fort Madison at the time. Then he adds, *"Hence, I am staying until spring where I am located"* and makes it plain that he will make arrangements to leave after receiving his *exeat* from Dubuque.

---

93 This may have been a reference to Psalm 102:20, which is "Pour entendre le gémissement des prisonniers, pour délier ceux qui étaient dévoués à la mort" or "To hear the groaning of the prisoner, To set free those who were doomed to death." [American Standard Bible] However, Galtier wrote "dévouée", which agrees with the feminine noun "victime", which can refer to either sex.

The last letter Galtier wrote to his bishop is dated January 13, 1845. It is quite a long one, provides the particulars of the Keokuk parish, and reiterates the determination to leave. *"I have been here more than seven months now. I cannot stay here to any advantage, my morale [virtue?] can't withstand the difficulty that I encounter here. I want to save myself; it is not to enter into disputes and get lost that I came to America...I would have never agreed to become a priest if I had understood that the obedience that I was promising was irrevocable and not reasonable in this sense, that I could never ask for its commutation or a change under the leadership of another superior and in another country nearer to my liking, my abilities, and my inclinations that I know now more than ever."*

Galtier also mentioned the $12.50 per month that Loras had apparently agreed to pay him, saying that he was tired of begging for it. It seems that Lucien had already communicated with the bishop of the diocese of Rodez in France, asking if he might be allowed to return there and place himself under that jurisdiction. Lastly, Galtier puts to Loras something he had recalled from his final days in the seminary there. *"Furthermore, another powerful reason which made me decide to come to America, is that in Rodez even the bishop had the goodness to repeat several times that he would send missionaries two by two, et misit illos binos."* [94]

In an earlier letter, Galtier had pointedly written: *"One should seek less to create a name for oneself and have a mission that is smaller in size but better sustained, and then the mission will prosper. A few years back, I could see what was starting to happen, and today without being a prophet, I believe that the mission work, unless it gets a different government, will lose even more."*

These remarks cannot have meant anything other

---

94 Latin for "He sent them out in pairs". Luke 10:1.

than that the missions of Dubuque, in spreading out, were spreading too thin. Some could neither be manned nor supported. While one cannot argue with Galtier's idea that pairs of missionaries, well-provided-for, could probably do a better job in fewer missions than lonely, starving ones scattered all over the great expanse of the diocese, this only works when the duos are compatible. As we have seen in the case of Ravoux and Godfert on the upper Mississippi and as we will further see, when Bishop Loras tried such an experiment, it tended not to be successful. It may even be that the bishop had told Galtier he could stay at Fort Madison with Allemann if he found Keokuk so objectionable, but a primarily German-speaking congregation was not the solution for a priest who spoke only French and English.

We have an indication that there was something more troubling Father Galtier than the state of the Iowa missions and Loras. In October he had already written to Mathias Loras that he should not be left "*exposed to a temptation so great where I risk my salvation, in a word, why leave me here, no longer useful to others and without receiving any help?*" But the source of the temptation is left vague. Also obscure is the point of telling the bishop, in December, "*I am, I confess sincerely, a great sinner, and often the memory of my iniquities comes to make me fear for my salvation.*"

There is a real possibility that Lucien may have reached a crossroads as far as the priesthood was concerned. He informed Loras that the "trial period" [as he had come to characterize it in his own mind] of being a missionary "*is now being turned into an eternity, as is the character of being an ecclesiastic. This surprises me greatly...*" It appears that Galtier was astonished at how much his zeal when it came to being a missionary, even a priest, had diminished in five years. Therefore, his wish to go back to Rodez is understandable. Either he would retrieve the enthusiasm of his seminarian days there—or he would not. Galtier, in writing that he wanted to save himself by leaving America, might have been really saying that he hoped to save his vocation. At any rate, his exact words to his superior were that he would rather work with his hands, earn his living by becoming a common laborer, than be a priest of the diocese of Dubuque.

Mathias Loras did not grant the *exeat*. The bishop was not in a good frame of mind, himself. He was beleaguered by all sorts of problems in the city of Dubuque, mostly caused by lay factions who wanted priests of their own national backgrounds, who spoke their own languages. Apparently, they wished to have parishes reflecting those they had left in Ireland or Germany. Matters came to a head when Loras was locked out of his own cathedral.[95] Disgusted, the bishop went into a kind of exile from Dubuque for a time, leaving matters to his vicar general, Father Cretin. Remaining for a while at Iowa City, Loras then went on to Burlington, removing a Father John Healy from his position as pastor there and taking his place. At least now Dubuque could be placated with the advent of an Irish priest. [Galtier's last letter to Loras was addressed to him at Burlington.]

This act of Loras worsened matters because, back in Dubuque, Healy allied himself with the extremist Irish dissenters, who were tired of French priests and prelates. Nevertheless, Father Healy got together with Antoine Godfert, now not a fan of Mathias Loras or his vicar general on account of having been judged to be in the wrong in his squabbles with Ravoux in Minnesota. These two priests commenced to behave boldly toward Father Joseph Cretin, the Frenchman left in charge—or so it was claimed.

Cretin, for his part, was suspicious of the visiting Father Mazzuchelli, who was well-liked by the Irish at Dubuque—some of them calling him "Father Matthew Kelly"—and feared the Italian might stir them up further

---

95 Source, Rev. Louis De Cailly, a grandnephew of Bishop Loras.

against the bishop. There was already opposition to the proposed cathedral, grumblings over costly repairs to the old one—and yet another voyage to France that Loras had planned. Apparently Lucien Galtier had saved enough money for his own passage to France and he left St. John the Evangelist a "widow", as he had warned he would.

Galtier had also threatened *"I shall write to France the necessary comment to my disappointment"*. Once he had departed Keokuk, Bishop Loras had no doubt he would go to Lyons and register his complaints about his superior in person. Loras, as evidenced by his letters, had previously written to the Society for the Propagation of the Faith, suspecting that someone or another was circulating unflattering rumors or complaints about him and entreating the Society to pay no mind. The nature of the supposed allegations was not specified, but where there is smoke there may have been fire and it might be that the bishop's suspicions were unfounded and merely fueled by his own pangs of guilt. Therefore, in order to defuse the situation with Galtier where the Society was concerned, Loras wrote the following to Lyons on the 19th of August, 1845:

"A young ecclesiastic named Lucien Galtier from Rodez must have passed through Lyons recently. He left Dubuque against the will of his superiors, although he might have done much good in the diocese. He had extremely exaggerated ambitions. He wanted 2,000 francs a year and a post of his own choice. I am convinced that you have judged him wisely. I beg his bishop to get him six months in the seminary to make him examine his conscience."

In the same missive, Loras tells the Society he needs more funds because he has allotted 15,000 francs *"to Mr. Cretin for his mission for the first year"*. Father Cretin was, at this time, to go once again among the Winnebago Indians, whereupon he encountered a number of difficulties. Cretin wrote to his brother in France in January of 1846: *"I have re-entered my solitude in the midst of the* savages from whom I will not depart until after Easter. I hope to succeed with a certain number. The inability of Protestantism to civilize these savages manifests itself more clearly day after day. It is a well-known fact that all those whom they had sought to civilize during twelve years have become more perverse than the others..."

It was not true that Galtier had demanded a "post of his own choice" as he had distinctly written to Loras that "*I don't see a single parish that would suit me*" [in Iowa].

During the absence of Lucien Galtier from America, the facts of which are mostly shrouded, we are freed from observing him long enough to discuss some things brought up in the last couple of paragraphs. There is something odd about one priest being thought undeserving of 2,000 francs per annum in order to minister to whites and half-breeds while another receives 15,000 to go among recalcitrant natives.

It is doubtful, however, that the Society was perturbed by the remarks of Bishop Loras against Galtier. They knew that 2,000 francs amounted to approximately 400 American dollars and that persons attached to other dioceses were probably earning as much. By 1844, Bishop John Henni of Milwaukee had applied to the Society for money with the help of Florimond Bonduel's expertise in French. Father Bonduel earned $420. at the Lake Poygan Indian mission and even Rosalie Dousman got $300. a year as a lay teacher there.[96]

Why civilizing the Indians was of such priority to Mathias Loras is not so understandable [other than that they still outnumbered the whites in some places] when he cannot have been insensible to the fact that the white citizens of the frontier towns in his diocese were not exactly

---

96 Johnson, Msgr. Peter Leo, *Crosier on the Frontier, A life of John Martin Henni* [Madison, 1959]. The local Indian Agent, John Suydam, "remarked that both teachers pronounced English imperfectly, especially the priest, but that in other respects his teaching was of high quality and his influence beneficial".

models of humane behavior, either. In the Midwest and farther west, lynchings were more common than trials and legal executions in the 19th Century. Vigilante "justice" was, in fact, out of control. Alcoholism, gambling and prostitution flourished all around. That drollest of writers, Walter N. Trenerry, author of *Murder in Minnesota*[97] created a book that is, in his own words, *"...a somber corrective to those adulators of the past who find every virtue in the crude life of the frontier."*

If Protestant ministers were accused of having failed to instill a reverence for the Ten Commandments in the Indians, let us now consider what became of some of the members of the family of Scott and Margaret Campbell, with whom Father Galtier found his first lodgings in the Minnesota Territory. The priest described Margaret as a good Catholic woman and one may suppose that all of her nine children were baptized and raised in that faith during the ministry of Galtier or his successor, Augustin Ravoux. As regards the sons of the couple, Baptiste was among the Indians executed for murder and various crimes at Mankato, Minnesota, in 1862 following an uprising or what is known as the Dakota War. What happened there is aptly described by militia commander, former Governor Henry H. Sibley[98] in a letter written September 8, 1862:

"I received a letter from Little Crow yesterday, by the two bearers of a flag of truce. He writes [his secretary is an educated half-breed] *that the reason the war was commenced was because he could not get the provisions and other supplies due the Indians, that the women and children were starving, and he could get no satisfaction from Major Gilbraith, the U.S. Agent. That he had many white women and children prisoners, etc., etc. I have sent the men back today with a written reply, telling Little Crow to deliver the captives to me, and that then I would walk with*

---
97 MHS Press, St. Paul [1962, 1985]
98 Minnesota joined the Union in 1858 and Sibley was its first state governor.

Henry H. Sibley

him like a man, etc., etc. What he will do remains to be seen. The half-breed bearers of the flag of truce, both of whom I know, say that the mixed bloods with their families are not permitted to leave the camp, and are virtually prisoners, as most of them are believed to sympathize with the whites. They assure me that the Indians are determined to give us battle, at or near the Yellow Medicine, and are sanguine of success. I sincerely hope they will not change their programme."

Little Crow did not release the captives and so, on September 23, there was "*a desperate fight of two hours* " after which General Sibley claimed victory, the militia having killed twenty-five or thirty of the warriors and wounded a large number. The opposing losses were reputedly considerably less. Another white flag was then sent over by half-breeds, with the Dakota asking to come and get their dead and also immunity from further punishment.

Little Crow

Sibley denied the request and subsequently moved right into the Indian encampment with his forces, freeing about a hundred and fifty white prisoners. Henry Sibley wrote to his wife that close to 400 of the surrendering warriors were taken captive. They were quickly tried and 392 were sentenced to death for crimes including murder and rape. But President Abraham Lincoln, that great humanitarian, reviewed the files on each Indian and ordered that only 39 of them be executed. Later one more was commuted, leaving 38 to be hung in Mankato, Minnesota, on December 26, 1862. Baptiste Campbell was among them. The priest who went to minister to the Catholics among the condemned was Augustin Ravoux.

The priest later wrote: *"Thirty-three died Catholics after having given such signs of faith, hope, and charity, contrition, and resignation to their unfortunate fate that I cannot entertain any doubt of their salvation."*

Little Crow, himself, was absent. The chief came back to Minnesota in 1863, where a white man and his son, hunting near Hutchinson, shot him. Sad to say, they received

$500 for his scalp from the state by way of bounty.

This was not the finest hour in Minnesota history by any means, with considerable wrong-doing on both sides, including the imprisonment of hundreds of Dakota women, children, and old men at Fort Snelling.

A man named Bishop Henry Whipple[99] decided to investigate why the Sioux had been so disgruntled as to start the hostilities in the first place. He wrote the following to Rev. Ezekiel Gear in 1862:  *"I spent several days in examining the books of the Indian bureau & my fears of dishonesty were all confirmed. The whole system is a bad one & in the hands of bad men as corrupt as can well can be. I had often heard the Indians complain of their wrongs but I hoped it was not just. In 1853 these Indians sold the Govt about 800 thousand acres of land. The lower Sioux's portion came to 96,000 [dollars]. A clause in this treaty states that these Indians shall go home & hold an open council & decide what shall be done with the money...years have lapsed since the sale...these Indians have never received a cent of that money...In June they came for the payment. They waited two months and no money came—mad, exasperated, starving—at last the outbreak came & it desolated 200 miles of our border...Deeply as I sympathize with our poor suffering [white] citizens, I do know that this war is justly due to robbery and wrong—and as I fear God, I will not keep silence. I have done all I could to arouse public attention to this matter & hope to do more."*

---

99 Whipple, born in 1822 in New York and dying in 1901 in Faribault, MN, became the Episcopalian bishop of Minnesota in 1859.

Another Campbell son, Hypolite, was also implicated in the Dakota uprising, but managed to save himself by fleeing to Manitoba. Scott Campbell Jr. died in an insane asylum but was never connected to any criminal offenses, being a quiet and harmless individual.[100]

Joseph Campbell, the eldest son, was likewise peaceful, but was forced to be present at the Yellow Medicine site by the Sioux, as the Campbell brothers were known to be the cousins of Little Crow. He was, however, absolved of partaking in any of the outrages and, moreover, was the man who wrote the letter from the chief of the Dakota to Sibley. The reason that Governor Sibley knew him and his brothers was that Sibley had lived at Mendota, being engaged in the fur business. His house there, quite a grand one for the time, still stands today as an historic monument. Joseph continued to be a resident of St. Paul after the battle. But the most famous or rather notorious of the brothers was John Campbell, born in 1832. John was a very handsome man with *"long, curly black hair, dark, expressive eyes, and a finely proportioned figure"*. His reputation for cruelty and licentiousness overshadowed his good attributes by far. His father, Scott, the Indian interpreter, had been known to like a tipple—but, as we are now only too well aware, that was nothing unusual around Fort Snelling in his day. Scott remained in the area for the rest of his life but died a pauper. Although once indispensable on account of his linguistic capability with both Sioux and Chippewa, in addition to French and English, Scott Campbell had become such a drunkard by 1843 that he had to be dismissed from his government position as interpreter for the Indian Agency. For this service he had received about 32 dollars a month, a very decent living at the time.

His boy John, though, was one of those people who seemed "born to be hung". He deserted from the army in

---

100 On his baptismal record, he appears to have been called "Mathias", after Bishop Loras. Indeed, Scott Jr. was baptized by the bishop on July 5, 1839, but the date of his birth was omitted for some reason.

1864 and nobody much regretted his leaving, John having been charged with murder and other crimes during his service. That same year the outlaw Campbell joined up with the Dakota, his paternal grandmother's people, and probably participated in the murder of the Jewett family near Mankato in May of 1865. When John was apprehended, he was wearing Mr. Jewett's trousers and two pairs of women's stockings. Campbell seemed impassive about the whole affair but managed to frighten the citizens of Mankato by claiming they were about to be attacked by the Sioux. He received a mock-trial, without representation, and was swiftly lynched by a Mankato mob. But the hanging was botched and John Campbell slowly strangled to death.

    His mother, Margaret, now living at Traverse des Sioux, received John's body and was terribly upset at what had happened to him. She did her best to rally the Dakota Nation into taking revenge and, fearing that she might succeed, Margaret was taken into custody by the authorities until she quieted down. Nothing happened to the killers of John Campbell, and it was recalled that they had briefly let him speak with a priest before the hanging. The Sioux did not fall upon Mankato at the time, although they complained bitterly about the lack of due process of law when it came to trying a half-breed. John Wilkes Booth had shot and killed Abraham Lincoln just a month previous to the incident at Mankato, Minnesota. The American Civil War, having begun in 1861, ended that same year.

    As for St. John the Evangelist of Keokuk, Galtier's place there was taken by Fr. Jean Villars, one of the seminarians who had been brought from France by Fr. Joseph Cretin following a visit there, and who was not ordained until 1848. Obviously, there had been a hiatus between resident pastors of the congregation, but others may have "visited it from time to time" as had been done previously and as Galtier had suggested to Loras was still the best solution for the time. Father Villars made some frame additions to the original log structure of St. John's and, in 1853, he brought the Visitation Sisters to Keokuk so that the town might have a Catholic school. Unfortunately, Father Villars may have lacked something as an administrator. He evidently concentrated too much on building up Visitation Convent for the nuns and didn't pay enough attention to church finances, failing to pay the taxes on the property he [or rather Loras] had bought for the parish. So it has been written, but it's also very possible that Villars simply couldn't raise the money. In 1855 Bishop Loras sent Father Wilhelm Emonds to assist Villars with a purse of 2,600 dollars in gold, but the property on Second and Blondeau Streets had already been lost. In due course, an acrimonious situation arose between the two priests.

This had to do with the fact that, as so often happened then, the congregation became divided into ethnic factions. The French probably would have sided with Father Villars in the beginning, but the Dutch and German Catholics of Keokuk had grown in number. They wanted Father Emonds and also a church of their own, for which they petitioned Loras. Villars, as was to be expected, protested strongly, but the bishop disregarded his objections and the cornerstone of the new church, St. Peter's, was laid. Its pastor, Father Emonds, proved energetic and popular. Soon St. John the Evangelist and the unhappy Fr. Jean Villars became abandoned by even the French faction. But, then, Lucien Galtier had warned, ten years before, that it was not the most united or dedicated group and had not done very much for him. After 1857, St. Peter's became the only Catholic church in Keokuk. Father Galtier's effort was torn down in 1861, the lumber being employed in the construction of a school behind the convent, but one of the additions of Villars, moved to Ninth and Johnson Sts., stood for 106 years until it was consumed by fire in 1967.

Father Villars was, unlike Galtier before him, evidently heartbroken by his removal from the town. Anticipating eventual defeat, he wrote these poignant words to Loras on the 8th of February, 1857: *"After nearly ten years in the missions of Iowa, and after all the services I have rendered for the diocese, have you finally decided what to do with me? Am I a good priest, or a bad one?"*

The rumor is that Jean Villars died by his own hand in 1868 after serving in the Indianapolis diocese for a few years. The archdiocese of Dubuque denies there is any proof of this alleged suicide. Father Emonds took Bishop Loras to task more than once for disregarding his complaints about Father Villars. In a letter from Keokuk dated Nov. 16, 1856, Emonds claimed to have been calumniated by a Rev. Heinrich Feddermann and so the situation had seemingly deteriorated even further with German priests now at odds. Feddermann had been accused of kissing a pregnant woman, which act he, himself, termed an "abomination" in a letter to Mathias Loras. Loras, fed up with the nonsense, forced the German to remain at his mission at Spruce Creek, even though he wanted to leave it.

Bishop John Henni of the Milwaukee Diocese

BEGINNING A NEW CHAPTER

If one credits astrology at all, it has already become apparent that Lucien Galtier had what is known as a Sagittarian personality. Among the traits he seems to have exhibited were volatility, being given to impatience, enthusiasm easily burned out lacking enough room for self-expression, being prone to a nervous disposition and ever ready to discard the old and move on to the new, a gift for eloquence, extroverted.

One of the new venues Father Galtier had in mind while still in Keokuk was serving in a convent. It was either that or a "well-organized parish". This he did not hesitate to disclose to Bishop Loras, who may have been quite surprised to read of the convent idea.[101] It does not require much imagination to conclude what Loras thought of the notion of a strong young priest, one who was actually not useless with his hands like so many of the others, wasting that ability in a convent. One can envision the bishop's eyes narrowing behind his spectacles as he perused the letter. There was so much to do in America and this rogue of a Galtier preferred to go back home and listen to the insipid secrets of a lot of nuns—or perhaps it was their simpering smiles he longed for! Maybe the sisters could embroider the initials L.G. on some linen handkerchiefs, which the malingerer could douse with eau de cologne and sniff

---

101 Galtier to Loras, November 8, 1844 "une paroisse bien réglée ou un couvent, voilà ma place..."

whenever he felt faint or feverish! Old priests were better suited to convents, no question there, and the sheer nerve of that enemy of the cross, Galtier, was pushing the patience of Loras to the limit. He was a bishop and yet he did his own sweeping and polished his own boots. Let Monsieur Galtier write as many complaining letters as he liked, waste his own money on paper and ink. The man was staying where he was and that was all there was to it.

What Mathias Loras may not have understood so well is that a person suffering from depression and who feels physically exhausted on account of it, longs for a refuge. Perhaps Lucien craved the gentle companionship of women or simply longed for a more tranquil, chaste environment than the town in which he found himself subjected to so much "scandalous behavior", as he surely would have put it. Moreover, one might gather from some of Father Galtier's comments to the bishop, that he no longer wished to be at the mercy of strangers, lay persons, even dreaded the idea. Young as he was, Galtier no longer trusted in his own health and strength and wanted someone dependable to look after him. The "bilious fever" that had attacked him in Minnesota and nearly taken his life haunted him whenever he felt unwell. A sudden tendency toward exaggerating every physical symptom is a well-known sign of depressive disorder. To Lucien, the Midwest now seemed a breeding-ground of pestilences, with miasmas hovering over each river town.

Joseph Cretin told Loras that he met a "Galtier" in Lyons in January of 1847, dubbing him "Monsieur Beaujolier" for some reason. But Cretin was referring to another Rev. Galtier, the spiritual director to an order of nuns. It is interesting to relate that the sisters of the Incarnate Word had their monastery on the hill of Fourviere, an old sector of Lyons. The order had been founded by Jeanne Chezard de Matel and more than 200 years later, in the year 1852, the nuns established themselves in Texas, a move that the founder could never have envisioned.

There was a priest associated with the diocese of St.Louis, who signed his baptismal entries "L. Galtier" [as Lucien always did] at St. Stephen's in Richwoods, Missouri, from December 24, 1846 until April 5, 1847. The St. Louis archives has a very small file on the reverend, but it does not include his first name. An analysis of that priest's penmanship, although of the French type, does not resemble that of Galtier, although the records can have been copied more recently. [Galtier returned in Nov. '46]

The fervently religious seem enigmatic to most others who are not inclined in that direction. Sometimes they are even a riddle to themselves. People who grow up in families where religion is a major theme with an emphasis on sin [during the 19th Century that encompassed a lot], tend to lean toward extremes. They either rebel against the lifestyle if they found it too oppressive or take up the theme, themselves, piety [or at least the external manifestations] having become an integral part of their personas. If they cannot always live up to the high standards set by their creed, they struggle with guilt as a result. However, they remain beings with human desires and, even though perhaps not consciously conflicted, subconscious struggles can result in some negative behavior or choices—even suicide. Inner conflict can make one very tired, even lead to emotional collapse. Add to that a life of hardship and the likelihood of chronic depression is not exactly nil.

That Father Galtier, in his those years prior to his fortieth birthday, evidenced some confusion as to what was the best path toward the holiness that was his conscious goal is already becoming plain. That he was not exactly happily self-sacrificing all of the time and could be a bit of an opportunist some of the time is not well-known because, in the past, it would not do to portray a priest as anything other than a saint. If he stayed away from the bottle and eschewed sexual expression, that was enough to qualify for "beyond reproach". But true saints are rare and Galtier, himself, never claimed to be one. His own opinion was that he was a sinner, although that assessment was probably too harsh. Like all other priests, Galtier was just a man, as glorious and as flawed as such a creation can be.

St. Paul's Archbishop John Ireland had written, in brief summary, the intriguing words: *"Father Galtier, on his removal from the north, was placed in charge of the missions at Keokuk, Iowa. In 1848 he returned to France, intending to spend there the remainder of his life. He had been strongly pressed to take charge of the French congregation of the Cathedral at St. Louis, but refused."*

For some reason, Galtier being urged to join the St. Louis diocese is suggested, but it is certainly not true that the priest waited until 1848 to return to France. The old city of St. Louis would not have been a good place to be in 1848. Late in the year, St. Louis was visited by a severe cholera epidemic, occasioning as many as 30 to 40 funerals a day at the cathedral alone! If that was not bad enough, a great fire swept through the downtown section of the city, killing three persons and doing millions of dollars worth of damage. Another "St. Louis" was the name of the cathedral of New Orleans, but it seems a different Galtier/Gautier was offered the position of assistant there in 1850 and not Lucien. If the latter was ever considered, nothing came of it.

Thomas McClean Newson wrote that cholera did not hit St. Paul until the year 1854 or 5, with several cases coming from the steamboats. *"I remember one poor fellow in the last stages of the disease, lying and apparently dying upon the ground, deserted. With a good Samaritan I went to him, gave him some whiskey, with powdered charcoal and sugar, and to the surprise of all he recovered. Years afterward he met me, hale and hearty, and his gratitude was unbounded."*

Amazing, indeed, but it became difficult, during this period, to obtain a facility for a cholera hospital. Due to the swift-acting course of the illness, it was so dreaded that few wished to be near the dying patients. However, that was the fate of Lucien Galtier's chapel at St. Paul, which by then had become a school of the sisters of St. Joseph—to be converted into such a hospital. In 1856 the chapel was dismantled; its logs numbered for reconstruction at St. Joseph's Academy. It was said that the wood was accidentally burned for warmth by some workmen who were unaware of its significance.

In June of 1847, Father Galtier arrived at Prairie du Chien, Wisconsin, another small river settlement—which never did grow much beyond a population of 6,000. Now he had joined the diocese of Milwaukee, headed by Bishop John Henni. He had remained in the land of his birth for a while and his activities while there are nebulous. It may be that Galtier had gone home to St. Affrique to be with his family. Perhaps he had merely needed to rest and regain his physical and mental vigor, or it may be that he had really examined his conscience at Rodez, as Mathias Loras had thought he should. But, certainly, it may be said that he had drunk of the water of the Mississippi and, as one had long ago returned to Egypt after once imbibing of the honey-flavored Nile, could not prevent himself from going back to the untamed American frontier.

Father Florimond Bonduel had been at Prairie du Chien but, by October of 1847 he was writing to a friend from Lake Poygan, Wisconsin, having been transferred there by Bishop Henni to work with the Menominee Indians. Bonduel knew how to communicate with them and Galtier did not, and it appears the bishop guessed wisely where each would be the more useful.

Regardless, it appears there was a chance that Henni may have wished to place Florimond Bonduel in St. Paul. In a letter to Olislagers de Meersenhoven in Belgium, the priest described his visit to "St. Peter's" and expressed disappointment with what he found there. *"The worldly state of the St. Paul mission is miserable,"* he lamented but did quantify the Catholics of the area as being

St. Gabriel's Church circa later 19th Century
Wisconsin Historical Society[102]

800 souls and made the telling observation that there were 20 families at Pig's Eye, indicating that the old name of the settlement had still stuck by 1846, the church of St. Paul not withstanding. Bonduel said a Sunday mass there and only remained a few days, setting out for the town of Stillwater. There *"...I grabbed a bell and went up and down the street calling people to come to worship. Within an hour I had gathered about fifty people and we assembled in a room loaned to me by a good Protestant. I gave instruction to them in English before going to bed."*

    Bonduel then made plans to establish a mission at Stillwater,[103] which he foresaw as having the potential to become a "great city" [it never did] and also one at St. Croix. Evidently he changed his mind and went back to Prairie du Chien where a letter from Bishop Henni awaited him. The prelate asked Father Bonduel to meet him at a place called Mineral Point where they could confer. Prior to the arrival of

---
102 Wisconsin Historical Society, image #42047
103 The church of St. Michael, founded in 1849, is probably the oldest Roman Catholic congregation at Stillwater.

A more current St. Gabriel's after considerable change to the exterior

Henni, Bonduel traveled about a bit, going to Madison [few Catholics there] and some other locations before suddenly falling gravely ill. "...*Excessive heat and fever almost took my life away in the midst of the burning sands of Wisconsin. I asked God to let me die and give one that crown of justice which he has promised to those who suffer for His glory, but my hour was not come. I had enough strength to take me as far as Milwaukee where the fatherly care of our Most Worthy Bishop hastened the return of my health.*"

Father Bonduel mentions to de Meersenhoven that it was he who had begun the first mission at Milwaukee in 1837 but that now there were three congregations there, a French, a German, and "*an English or American*". Bonduel estimated the Catholic population of Milwaukee at not less than 7,000. Having reclaimed his health, the priest and Bishop Henni made a tour of various places in northern Wisconsin and then Bonduel settled down at Lake Poygan for a considerable length of time, beginning in late 1846.

PRAIRIE DU CHIEN

The church that Father Galtier came to was called St. Gabriel Archangel and it still exists today, having been in continuous use all this time. The cemetery behind the church is populated with some of Prairie du Chien's early Catholics.

The town of Prairie du Chien is located in southern Wisconsin on the western border where the Mississippi and Wisconsin rivers converge. It is the seat of Crawford County where the trial of Edward Phelan had been held. So now Lucien Galter was about 300 miles south of where he had begun but considerably farther north of Keokuk. The beginnings of the settlement are by now predictable. A French trading post had been established there in 1685, consisting of some structures huddling inside a stockade for protection against the Indians. Jonathan Carver was there in 1766, finding a large tribe of Fox Indians. Since the chief's name was Alim or "Dog", Carver called the surrounding prairie "Dog Plain" but the French residents changed that to "Prairie du Chien."

In the 19th Century, Prairie du Chien's foremost fur traders were Joseph Rolette, Nathan Myrick, and Hercules L. Dousman. The latter, particularly, made a fortune in the fur trade, which combined with other types of investments, caused him to become Wisconsin's first millionaire. In 1844, two years after the death of Joseph Rolette Sr., Hercules Dousman married his former partner's wife, Jane [or Genevieve], daughter of Henry Fisher and Madeleine

Gauthier de Verville. Miss Fisher had been given as a bride to Joe Rolette at the age of thirteen. The groom was thirty-eight.

Hercules L. Dousman[104]

Dousman died in 1868, and his son, H. Louis Dousman, inherited much of his wealth. In 1870 the heir built a grand Victorian mansion over the site of the former Fort Shelby. When Louis died unexpectedly in 1886, his family renamed the home "Villa Louis" in his memory. It still stands and is a tourist attraction of the area.

Prairie du Chien was the place of a battle over control of Fort Shelby and the fur concession, involving the Americans and the British. This happened in the year 1812 and was the only war between two countries fought in

---

104 Wisconsin Historical Society, image #2620

Wisconsin. Fort Shelby was burned, but was replaced by Fort Crawford in 1816.

In 1825, 1829 and 1830 important treaties were signed with the area nations, the Sauk and the Fox, at Fort Crawford. When this wooden fort was destroyed by flooding, the second Fort Crawford was erected from stone. In 1832 Black Hawk, a chief of the Sauk Indians, surrendered to Colonel Zachary Taylor, ending the Black Hawk War that had lasted four months. The reader will recall that Virginia Wilcox's father was involved in this conflict. Crawford was abandoned and troops removed in 1856, but the fort was once again put to use during the Civil War, as was Fort Snelling.

Joseph Rolette, Junior

Some of the magnates of the fur trade at Prairie du Chien had connections with Minnesota. Joseph Rolette Sr. and Hercules Dousman had as their business partner Henry H. Sibley, future governor of the state. Joseph Rolette Jr., son of the elder and his wife, Jane,[105] became a politician and a member of the Legislature there. Nathan Myrick, born in New York, afterward came to La Crosse, Wisconsin, and was a founder of that town, establishing a fur trading post there, too. Myrick was engaged in the lumber business around the year 1849, when he moved to St. Paul for good. H. Louis Dousman, son of Hercules and Jane, married Nina Linn Sturgis in St. Paul in 1872. Euphrosine Powers, daughter of the man who donated the ground for St. Gabriel's Church, married Thomas Leblanc, also known as Thomas Provençal, a French-Sioux guide who originated from around Fort Snelling. Emilie Rolette, a daughter of Joseph Sr., was wed to Captain Alexander Hooe, who was stationed at that same garrison but later at Fort Crawford.

Father Samuel Mazzuchelli had come to Prairie du Chien in 1832. He recollected that: *"...This village, according to an old tradition, bears the name of a chief called "The Dog", whose tribe inhabited that immense prairie which follows the Mississippi for many miles, with a chain of hills to the east. Situated at the mouth of the Wisconsin River, it had been for about a century a post of great importance for the traders in their traffic with the different tribes...*

The Catholics of Prairie du Chien were visited from time to time by Priests, who used to come from the city of St. Louis in the state of Missouri by ascending the great river for almost six hundred miles."

Mazzuchelli said mass in an ordinary house and attempted to persuade the resident Catholics to build a church. When nothing could be organized, the Dominican went away. There wasn't much he could do, as he was then living at Mackinac Island, about 400 miles from Prairie du Chien. However, on a subsequent visit in 1836, while posted at Galena, Illinois [the lead mining district] Mazzuchelli received the donation of a lot from an individual

---

105 Rolette Jr. was born in 1820 when his mother was merely 15 or 16. Jane was married to Dousman on Dec. 26, 1844 by Father Bonduel.

called Strange Powers. It is likely Father Mazzuchelli who chose the name for the proposed church, whose cornerstone was not laid until 1839 by Bishop Mathias Loras. Loras still had jurisdiction over western Wisconsin at that date.

The paper, the *Wahrheits-Freund*, published the following: *"The good people of that place which is so beautifully situated at a junction of the Wisconsin and Mississippi rivers, were greatly delighted to see a Bishop in their midst for the first time. They earnestly sought that he tarry with them several days. So it befell, and a series of spiritual exercises, coupled with a thorough course of instructions, was begun at once. The Catholics, almost 700 souls, nearly all French, availed themselves of this opportunity for their spiritual welfare; 86 persons were led to the table of the Lord, 52 were confirmed, 19 were baptized, and 24 marriages were blessed...a collection for the church building was ordered by the Bishop, who himself first placed a gold coin in the collection, which soon amounted to $105. The church is to be begun at once, is to be 100 feet long, 50 feet wide, and of Gothic style."*[106]

Mazzuchelli, one of the wandering or "circuit priests", made continuing visits to the parish and tried to oversee the building of the church. This was a busy time for the ubiquitous Milanese. His further remarks about St. Gabriel's are: "*The stone work is done by Mr. L. R. Marsh, who deserves much credit for his exertions. The carpenter work is in the hands of a good son of Erin, Mr. Benedict F. Manahan, whose zeal for the temple of God knows no obstacle, and whose knowledge of the trade will be sufficiently praised by his work.*

...The walls are two feet thick above the base, built of the good and light stone, found in abundance on the hills which encircle the majestic prairie between the junction of the great Wisconsin River and the Father of Waters.

---

106 Issue of September 5, 1839.

The style of the church is a chaste Gothic: the front is all hammered range work, ornamented with a marble inscription and niche. The fact that it is being built on a gentle swelling of the prairie adds much to the appearance; the houses and farms, scattered up and down, east and west, on the vast fertile plain receive already a peculiar beauty by the presence of God's holy tabernacle, and remind us of the plains over which the Ark of the Covenant traveled, surrounded by the tents of the children of Israel.

It is noteworthy that the first church built in the oldest settlement on the eastern boundary of the Wisconsin Territory, that is, at Green Bay, was a Catholic one; and the first one on the western boundary is a Catholic one also. The Cross of Christ has within the last four years been planted in many places on the west shore of the Mississippi, and most certainly advancing with a divine step through all the beautiful regions of the Territory of Iowa, will soon, like a new star, make its glittering appearance on the shores of the Upper Missouri. Let us pray God to send many good laborers into His vineyard."

Antoine Pelamourgues arrived at Prairie du Chien to briefly lend Father Mazzuchelli a hand but, after Augustin Ravoux was ordained, the latter went there, instead. It was now 1840 and St. Gabriel's had not yet been completed, its debts slowly mounting.

As the reader will recall, Ravoux did not remain long among this congregation, being transferred to the Minnesota waters in 1841 in order to convert the natives. Father Joseph Cretin took the post at St. Gabriel's and, in 1843, Augustin Ravoux paid a visit to Prairie du Chien in order to use Cretin's printing press for the purpose of creating a religious booklet in the Sioux language. Ravoux returned to his Minnesota Indians, Cretin soon leaving, as well. In December of 1844, Father Jean Claude Perrodin arrived at St. Gabriel's, to remain for but the blink of an eye, but the Latin language records of Florimond Bonduel, who evidently came in the summer of 1844, continue until 1846. Jacques Causse, the young seminarian whom Lucien Galtier "fortified" for the American missions while they were both still studying in France, and who had defected to the Milwaukee diocese by this time, took up the pastoral duties at St. Gabriel's in December of 1846, remaining until Galtier relieved him in 1847.[107]

What made St. Gabriel's parish, located within a river town, so much more acceptable to Lucien Galtier than the incipient St. Paul or Keokuk is not difficult to surmise. The main reason may have been that the parish already had a substantial number of Catholics and to complete that partial church presented a challenge. Father Bonduel, in a letter to a friend, written in 1847, gave his impression of the town and the church in which he had served:

"*Prairie du Chien, a former French colony, is a town of 1200 to 1500 souls. During the two years I remained there I opened two missions, 10 or 12 miles from the city, one at Patch Grove and the other to the south of the Kickapoo river. There are about 1,000 Catholics within the limits of this circumference. The city of Prairie du Chien itself is one of the most beautifully situated on the upper Mississippi river and is located near the mouth of the Wisconsin river...There is a very beautiful church built in stone, but not yet finished...In addition to the church there is a pretty chapel and a rectory which I built there...*"[108]

Now Galtier had a rectory in which to live and probably even his own horse because he was to cover a lot of territory. However, it would seem that St. Gabriel's did not

---

[107] It would appear that all of the original missionaries brought from France by Bishop Loras in 1838 were posted at Prairie du Chien at one time or another. However, none came close to staying as long as Galtier did.

[108] This was not the rectory that still stands to the south of the church and it's not clear what Bonduel meant by what he built, as a frame house, including a chapel, appears to have already been occupied by Father Cretin. Bonduel died at Green Bay on Friday the 13th of December, 1861. He was 62 years old.

yet have a roof. This meant that, in fair weather, masses could be said in the church but, on other days, the chapel, mentioned by Bonduel, had to suffice.

Jane Dousman[109]

Another presumable advantage of St. Gabriel's was becoming the confessor of the "grande dame" of Prairie du Chien, the lovely, French-speaking Jane Dousman, who could hardly fail to become a benefactress to the only priest in her town. However, it is difficult to know to what extent Jane could have met with Father Galtier's approval, as it was common knowledge in Prairie du Chien that she had fallen

---

109 Wisconsin Historical Society, item #2622

in love with the good-looking, ambitious Hercules while still the wife of Joe Rolette. In those unforgiving times, Jane would have been considered "tainted", regardless of her husband's success. Hopefully, Lucien Galtier had sufficiently matured by then to find understanding in his heart for Mrs. Dousman.

It also appears that the Bishop of Milwaukee, John Henni, who now had jurisdiction over western Wisconsin, was a man with whom Galtier could deal more easily than with Mathias Loras. Likewise, Father Galtier seems to have earned the respect of Henni, who appreciated his talents.

St. Gabriel's church was intended, from the outset, to have been a grander affair than the homely log chapels in the domain of Loras, due to the idea of the latter that Prairie du Chien would become an episcopal see. Therefore, Galtier inherited a stone church building that could not be completed due to the poverty of the congregation—and still had not been by 1849—with a debt of 3,000 dollars hanging over it, a very considerable sum for its day and place.[110]

It was in that same year that Bishop Henni and Galtier collaborated in what was a rather desperate plan. Galtier would go among the large French Catholic population of New Orleans and ask for donations so that, at least, the outstanding debt of the parish could be paid. No fool, Henni realized that the distinguished, charismatic Galtier was the ideal person to loosen the purse strings of the southerners. A man who appeared so noble, so erudite, but was in charge

---

110 It would seem that the Dousman and Rolette families belonged to the parish but Joe "King" Rolette had lost his fortune previous to his death in 1842 and his wife, as well, they having become separated. Hercules Dousman did not gain the bulk of his own wealth until around 1852 when he became a principle investor in the Madison & Prairie du Chien Railroad, later the Chicago, Milwaukee, St. Paul & Pacific Railroad. Dousman deeded the land for a new cemetery, named Calvary, to St. Gabriel's sometime previous to 1861, replacing the old "French Cemetery". He and other Dousmans are buried near the center of Calvary.

of such a poor congregation could not help but move them to charity. But, of course, Galtier could not go there without the sanction of the Right Reverend Anthony Blanc, Bishop of New Orleans.

Therefore, on November 2nd of 1849, John Henni wrote Blanc a letter that included the following sentiments with reference to St. Gabriel's and its pastor: *"...hence the large stone building which still lies like an incubus upon the poor people & every priest I send there...but all I could do would be [at] the utmost to pay the interest. I therefore asked the good pastor to try his best by collection. It's the first time, as poor as we are here, that I allowed any of my priests to make collections out of my Diocese. But in this case being more urgent than any other can be—I could not refrain from doing or allowing what I otherwise do not wish.*

Be pleased, then, Rt. Reverend Brother, not to take it amiss in seeing Father Galtier in your midst. He is a truly worthy priest & and as such he deserves your protection— whilst I hope that you will not think it too great an intrusion on our part..."[111]

Although numerous, the Catholics of New Orleans were not without their own worries. There were outbreaks of Yellow Fever each year between 1817-1905. In 1849 there were 769 recorded deaths from the disease but only 107 in 1850. During some years the fatalities amounted to thousands.

Father Joseph Cretin received notice from Rome, in September of 1850, of his appointment as the first bishop of the new diocese of St. Paul. Lucien Galtier continued the struggle to complete St. Gabriel's. In April of 1849 he had advertised in the Prairie du Chien *Patriot* newspaper the commencement of the sale of pews. This meant that members of the congregation would have their own seats in the church reserved for their families. Old lists of the people who paid for these pews still exist at the church today.

---

111 University of Notre Dame Archives, Archdiocese of New Orleans Collection.

An 1850 census has Galtier living with a Scottish woman named Penelope McLeod as his housekeeper. Lucien was thirty-eight at that time and Penelope, a single female, gave her age as only thirty-three, too young for a church that prefers post-menopausal live-ins.[112] How long Penelope remained Galtier's housekeeper is not clear, but they continued to be friends for the rest of his life. There were other housekeepers in the interim, including the Irish-born Anne Fitzpatric [sic on the 1860 census].

Father Galtier had finally acquired what he had told Bishop Loras he thought he deserved while at Keokuk—someone to look after him. Yet one could hardly say he lived the life of a parish priest of France. It was still the American frontier and Prairie du Chien was a far cry from a bucolic European village. While the local druggist sold "French Perfumery" in addition to patent medicines, there were also "guns and pistols" available for purchase in his shop. By 1847, the year of the arrival of Galtier, things had settled down considerably, however, particularly where the troubles with the Indians was concerned. Back in 1814, trader Joe Rolette's relative, Antoine Dubois, the brother of his first wife, was murdered by the Dakota. He and another man, Louis Champagnie, were shot. The latter died instantly, but Dubois, still a young man, managed to travel twenty-four miles before expiring.

In 1826 the entire Methode family, including five children, had been murdered while gathering maple sugar by some Winnebago tribesmen. A year later, Registre Gagnier and Solomon Lipcap, a man who worked for him, were killed by others of that nation. Even Gagnier's infant daughter was scalped and left for dead, but the baby miraculously survived and lived to a good age.

In the meantime, the difficulties of Bishop Loras with

---

112 Penelope McLeod, whose grave marker in Calvary Cemetery states she was born in 1815, was actually 35 to Galtier's 38 years. In 1918 Canon Law decreed that housekeepers must be "above the age of suspicion". Penelope was the sister-in-law of attorney, Leander LeClerc, a neighbor.

his priests continued. Fr. John Allemann had contracted some debts and Loras, to avoid a legal scandal in which the Alsatian priest was threatening to become embroiled, paid off the man's arrears. This lightened Allemann's load but, in 1847, he wrote to Loras, stating, "*I am doing well and would be better if your Lordship would open his purse strings.*" In 1849 Allemann was still complaining to his bishop about his financial woes. But by 1851 Allemann had transferred out of Dubuque to the Chicago diocese, as Remigius Petiot had done before him. The reason for the transfer is not clear. Father Alexander Hattenberger, who was Allemann's successor at Fort Madison, would write Loras in strong language demanding better support. John Allemann died at St. Vincent's Sanitarium in St. Louis in 1865, the cause of death being entered as "melancholia".

A young Samuele Carlo Mazzuchelli

In February of 1846 Loras informed the Society at Lyons that Samuel Mazzuchelli no longer belonged to his diocese but that of Bishop Henni. Loras cautioned the organization not to give any funds to this priest unless it could be cleared up whether the money was going to be used for the benefit of the Dominicans and not "a private institution". Considering how hard Mazzuchelli had worked for the Iowa missions all the years since coming to America in his twenties, this communication seems quite petty.

In the same year Bishop Loras wrote to Anthony Blanc of New Orleans that he had given an *exeat* to that very Father John Healy he had sent to Dubuque from Burlington to placate the Irish, but who had ended up doing just the opposite. He tells Blanc that he has granted the release *"in order to avoid scandal and a kind of schism"* and hopes that Blanc would give him information in a similar case. Perhaps Loras was suggesting that the bishops should create a kind of "database" of rebel clerics so as to be forewarned in the event of their migration. Bishops are not supposed to accept priests who had not received *exeats* from previous dioceses, but it seemed John Henni of Milwaukee was not so scrupulous in following this church rule.

By 1847, Mathias Loras had fourteen churches but only seven missionaries. An interesting letter dated March 14, 1849 has Loras writing to Bishop Ignatius Bourget of Montreal, asking for some financial help for a Father Belcourt at Pembina in what is now the northeastern corner of North Dakota. At the time, Pembina fell under the jurisdiction of Dubuque.[113] Loras claimed that the Society was about to cut off its subsidy completely and wondered if it would be possible for him to travel to the principal Canadian cities for the purpose of soliciting funds. In reply, Bourget, himself, pleaded poverty and even chided Loras for his request. On April 3, 1849 Loras thanked the Society For the Propagation of the Faith for the sum of 6,420 francs received on the second of February! In July of 1850, the bishop forwarded a pleading letter to the Society from what seems to have been his new "poster boy" of priestly

---

113 It took Father Belcourt's letters four to six weeks to reach Bishop Loras, having to cross the prairies from *"Dakota, through Minnesota to Fort Snelling, and down the Mississippi..."* M. M. Hoffmann, p. 217.

privation, the same Fr. Georges Belcourt, stationed 600 miles to the north of Dubuque, the most distant point of the diocese. Loras was writing to France from his "summer home", Mt. Saint Bernard, a farm he had bought in 1849, later to become the site of a seminary. On October 24 another letter of Belcourt was employed in the same fashion. Father Belcourt was absorbed into the new diocese of St. Paul in 1857.

What sort of place was Mt. Saint Bernard? Any question on the part of the curious can be answered by a letter Bishop Loras wrote to his brother in January of 1851:

"*Every Thursday I go to Mt. Saint Bernard to rest, or rather to read, and write more freely than in Dubuque. It is a truly magnificent farm, a field of 113 acres, four horses, two oxen, six cows, five calves, fifty hens, twelve ducks, three turkeys, thirty-two sheep, 150 acres of woods, swine, etc., etc. The four servants receive twenty-five piastres a month in all, and board. I have planted 200 poplars from Italy. A hundred apple trees will be planted in the spring. It would be a great pleasure for me to spend my time here peaceably, having a school and a chapel. I have to feed 25 people and the farm products help. Besides this, we have the St. Mathias farm, four miles distant. We rent it for $150 a year, and it is no problem...We have a third farm, St. Mary, rented at $80. It will be the legacy of my old age...*"

In 1851 Father Jean Claude Perrodin wrote his letter of farewell to Loras, doubtless hoping for more favorable conditions under Bishop Henni. Perrodin, who has a role in the final scene of the life of Lucien Galtier, came to Dubuque toward the end of 1841. As it happened, Perrodin had an uncle, the superior of a college in France, who wrote to Loras, asking him to watch over his nephew. In the same letter, this uncle advised the bishop that Jean Claude was "*very young, volatile, and of an easygoing disposition.*" It seemed to the uncle that this young man would greatly benefit from "*the heroic courage*" of his friend, Godfert, "*whose departure to a far distant mission has much edified us."* Godfert had left the Dubuque diocese some years previous to Perrodin's exit.

Another priest, Father Benoit Poyet, also left in 1851. Loras had a few words to say about about him to Bishop Blanc, actually gave him a recommendation: *"He has ministered in Iowa City for more than three years. He has lived at the cathedral for several months and his conduct has been beyond reproach. However, the appointment does not suit him. I asked him to select any place in our diocese which might be acceptable to him. He wishes to leave. I could not refuse him an exeat. I have asked him to see you about securing a satisfactory post. A conversation of a quarter of an hour either in French or in English with this ecclesiastic will show you what he is. He also knows a little German. He is well-mannered, has a beautiful voice, and preaches very well in English, so that I think he can succeed very well anywhere you place him."*

How different the attitude of Mathias Loras toward Father Poyet, who wished to remain under his jurisdiction no more than Galtier had! This young man was offered any spot in the diocese, yet Lucien had been reviled to the Society for supposedly wanting *"a post of his own choice"*, when the truth was that he wanted out of the Iowa missions for good.

From then on, Loras began to acquire non-French additions to his diocese. The Society For the Propagation of the Faith continued to send francs to the Bishop of Dubuque.

Father Joseph Cretin, the supreme "fair-haired lad" of Loras from the outset, only left the bishop to become one, himself. In 1839, Loras had described him to Blanc as *"an angel of piety, kindness and courtesy, and who is very discrete."* At one point, Cretin had entertained the idea of following a group of pioneers to California, but failed to get the permission of Loras. The priest wrote to his sister in the spring of 1849: *"You see, my dear sister, that I am still at Dubuque. The colony of our people who are going to*

California departed yesterday. Msgr. Loras did not allow me to accompany them; or rather he thought it his duty to assure me that I should act against the will of God if I left Dubuque. I had to yield. May God's will be done. I think it will be to my advantage. The journey would no doubt involve many hardships but I shall not be without troubles where I am. The Bishop leaves tomorrow to be absent more than five months. I shall be here alone; cholera is approaching our city. It is not very agreeable to to be called at any moment to a distance of some five or six miles, night or day, and to travel over impassable roads."[114]

    Outside of Cretin, Ravoux, and Pelamourgues, not one other of the original priests of the diocese remained, for one reason or another. Augustin Ravoux, who was to become vicar general of the new diocese of St. Paul, never intentionally broke with Loras, although he might easily have asked to join Bishop Henni. Even though the St. Paul congregation that he served, which was in the domain of the Milwaukee diocese, was much larger than his other one at Mendota, Ravoux seems to indicate that he remained with Dubuque, visiting the see every year. It appears rather ironic that a Catholic priest, one who became a monsignor and so well known in St. Paul, claimed, in his autobiography, to have begged the Bishop of Milwaukee to send another priest for the city, but none could be spared. Perhaps Ravoux simply wanted to spend more time with the Indians, but Henni most likely found it convenient to let him do what he had been doing for the faithful of St. Paul.

    If the reader had already made up his mind about the character of Bishop Mathias Loras, he ought to know that the bishop was not hard-hearted and could be quite tolerant at times, even if he suspected a missionary might be less than a rock of sanity. Father Allemann had been accused of emotional instability and had even been dropped by his

---

114 Cretin to France, April 12, 1849, copy in the St. Paul Seminary Library.

Dominican order, but his depressions did not preclude him from being a generous priest and even working himself into a premature old age. Had there been something dangerous about John Allemann, Loras would have doubtless come down on him as hard as he did certain intemperate clerics within his diocese. At least one hopes so. In trying to make sense of all the difficulties Bishop Loras encountered with his priests, or at least a fair number of them, the author has received the impression that all concerned had "bitten off more than they could chew" in some fashion.

There can be no doubt that Mathias Loras was sincere about wanting to convert the Indians and to establish Catholicism as firmly and widely as possible within his see by the erection of the chapels wherever the faithful could be found. Even though Loras had once promised to pay his missionaries a stipend of at least ten dollars a month for their upkeep, there simply wasn't enough income to support all of the bishop's plans at all times. Therefore, some rather naïve expectations were relied upon. Loras probably was convinced that the Catholics in the scattered communities of the frontier would do all they could to help the priests and keep them from going under out of charity. Were they not there for the benefit of the congregations and their immortal souls? In certain cases there was charity, as we now know, but most of the Catholics were poor, themselves, and had, moreover, heard rumors of the great wealth of the church of Rome. They may have felt that the ultimate responsibility for the missionaries lay with the Pope, who had, after all, created the diocese and appointed the bishop.

Also, Loras possibly overestimated the devotion of the wilderness Catholics to their faith. Many of them had disregarded it for years because they had lived so long without church bells to remind them even of the fact that it was Sunday. And some had discovered that life continued well enough without priests and masses. The Indian girls the men had chosen to live with did not require a wedding band or words spoken by an abbé to make them into faithful wives. Moreover, dedication to religiosity had never been the domain of the average French male.

The missionaries, for the most part, were quite young when Loras brought them to America. He had become, in effect, a kind of father-figure for them and they trusted him to be watchful over their well-being, despite realizing that their lives would not be easy. When they came to feel neglect, they at first wrote quite piteously to the man upon whom they depended and later with disenchanted rancor. One can imagine the young men, in their wretchedness, envisioning Monseigneur the Bishop living in careless comfort at Dubuque, dreaming of successes and honors for himself. That they, also, had bitten off too large a portion lay in the fact that some of them were simply not physically strong enough, sufficiently resourceful, or optimistic to the point where they could bear their burden without cracking. They were probably also not as emotionally or socially mature for their age as they might have been, not having undergone the rites of passage of other young males and the responsibility that came with all that. The seminaries had provided them with food and lodging and had isolated them from the company of all but their own kind. Some were not much accustomed to physical labor, had never held any sort of job or ever made their own decisions. In some cases, even the decision to become a priest had not been their own. In those days boys could be given over to the seminary by their relatives without their consent. By the time they grew to manhood, it became the only sort of life they knew. Yet, for the most part, these young Europeans matured under their harsh circumstances in the New World, toughened up, discovering inner resources they never knew they possessed. Some even found their element, perhaps even causing people to conclude that God works in mysterious ways.

  A prime example of this last was Fr. Samuel Mazzuchelli, the lad from a wealthy Italian family, whose "delicate" portraits both as a youth and in middle-age would never cause anyone to suspect him of being the ideal pioneer padre. Far more robust than he appeared, Mazzuchelli maintained his perfect manners and bonhomie together with an unflagging energy, lending the impression that the American frontier was exactly where he belonged and he had always known it, going there as soon as he could. By contrast, Lucien Galtier, who looked like he might actually have had some hair on his chest, had the strength to do hard physical work, was not nearly as resilient or adaptable as Mazzuchelli or Augustin Ravoux, the man who was comfortable wearing deerskin. Ravoux was a born story-teller, and he wrote extraordinarily long letters, having an even more ornate handwriting than Galtier. Also, Mazzuchelli and Ravoux both took the trouble to pen real autobiographies, while Galtier unfortunately did not.

It has long since been recognized—and should have been at the time by anyone with even a small understanding of humanity— that one simply should not send a missionary anywhere, let alone to a remote, untamed, location by himself. Few persons can withstand that much lack of moral, emotional, and physical support and that is a separate issue from a shortage of amenities. As soon as Lucien reached the conclusion that Bishop Loras was making the burden heavier than necessary, he lost his respect and, before long, Galtier made that quite obvious. And the bishop's rather effeminate response of wounded feelings accompanied by tears probably only heightened Galtier's contempt.

Father Galtier, too, seemed to indicate that one of the things he missed most was the presence of another priest. Even today, some priests complain that they can find little common ground with lay persons when it comes to socializing, so one can well imagine the gulf between someone like the intellectual Galtier, when he first came to St. Peter's, and those other card playing, blaspheming, whiskey drinking men around Fort Snelling. No wonder that the fortuitous visit of a traveling French bishop seemed to Galtier like the apparition of an angel of mercy.

In summary, the propagation of Catholicism along the Mississippi river was based upon faith, hope, and a good measure of abdication of responsibility. That it succeeded at all—and it did, of course—was due to tenacity, dedication, and tremendous sacrifice evidenced by those pioneer priests over the long haul. Some of them may have divorced themselves from Mathias Loras, but most remained on the frontier, regardless. Loras died on February 19, 1858 in Dubuque, at the age of 65, following a brief illness. Whatever the virtues or flaws of his personal character, his ability as an administrator must be critically questioned.

Father Joseph Cretin[115]

THE FATE OF RAVOUX AND CRETIN

As the reader has already seen indications of the future success of both Joseph Cretin and Augustin Ravoux in Minnesota, we can allow Ravoux to tell the tale best in his own words:

"From the departure of Father Galtier, in the spring of 1844, till 1851, excluding the time of my two excursions to the Missouri River, and a few days I spent in Dubuque every year, I alternately resided in Mendota and St. Paul. For about three years, I was two consecutive Sundays in Mendota and the third one in St. Paul, preaching every Sunday in the French and English languages when at Mendota, doing the same at St. Paul as soon as we had in

---

115 Minnesota Historical Society Collections.

our congregation some members who did not understand the French, but this was not before 1848 or 1849. In 1847 we had to make an addition to the chapel of St. Paul, erected by the Rev. Father Galtier, in 1841. The small chapel used by the Sisters of St. Joseph, till their removal to St. Joseph's Academy, formed the addition. In 1849 the chapel was again too small, and many of the faithful had to remain standing outside during the divine service. A great portion of the members of the Catholic church who overcrowded the chapel on Sundays, were not only those living in St. Paul, but many from Little Canada, St. Anthony, and Mendota, with others who resided two or three miles along the left bank of the Mississippi.

In 1847 the Catholic population becoming more numerous at St. Paul and around it than at Mendota and Fort Snelling, I had, then, the divine service in St. Paul every second Sunday. In 1849, the Catholics still continuing to increase on the east bank of the Mississippi, and yet unable to have a priest from the diocese of Milwaukee, I determined upon spending two Sundays in St. Paul, and the third one in Mendota. I wrote again to the Rt. Rev. Bishop of Milwaukee, describing to him the great wants of the Catholic population in this part of his diocese, and spoke to him on the necessity of sending a priest to reside in St. Paul. In my letter I urged him so much to provide for that portion of the flock entrusted to his care by Divine Providence, that, before terminating it, I thought it my duty to excuse myself for the liberty of my remarks.

In his answer to me the good and pious bishop began his letter by these words: 'I heartily forgive you for the kind lecture you read to a bishop; you are perfectly right, but you ought to be aware of the trouble, nay, the impossibilities on the other side.' Then the Right Rev. Bishop expresses his hope that, before long, a new diocese would be established for the Territory of Minnesota, and that St. Paul would be the place selected for the bishopric. The date of that letter is January 31st, 1850.

Late in the autumn of the same year, the bulls were sent from Rome to the Very Rev. Joseph Cretin; he had been elected bishop of St. Paul. I had the honor of receiving from him a letter which would have caused me the greatest pleasure had it not been for his indecision about accepting the charge. In his letter he told me that he was about to start for Europe, and that no determination would be taken by him for some time. He asked me to give him my advice on the acceptation or refusal of the new bishopric. Such a question surprised me very much. In my answer I pressed him to accept, showing him, by many reasons, how very necessary it was for the Catholics of this territory. I urgently requested him to come to St. Paul before his departure for Europe, in order to buy a location for his cathedral, informing him that entire blocks, in a suitable place, began to be scarce; that perhaps, at his return, he could not find any except by paying a very high price. I did all in my power to encourage him to accept the bishopric offered to him. I went so far as to tell him in my letter, that things were in such a condition in this new territory that, according to my opinion, he was obliged, sub gravi, to give his consent to bear the load imposed upon him by Divine Providence.

He wrote to me a second letter, but leaving me yet in great doubt whether he would or would not accept the charge. After his departure for France, aware of the necessity of securing some lots for the cathedral and other purposes, I bought of Mr. Vital Guerin twenty-one lots for $800, and for $100 the lot on which now stands the cathedral. This last I bought of another person, who had already some lumber on the ground for a building. He had bought the same on credit of Mr. Vital Guerin for $60. He ceded me that lot for $40 profit. I considered the purchase of the twenty-two lots a very good bargain for the church, as also a good one for Mr. Vital Guerin, because it was understood that the cathedral and other buildings would be erected on block seven, and such improvements would increase the value of Mr. Vital Guerin's property. The event proved that I was not deceived in my expectation. The Right Rev. Bishop after his return from France, paid the money for the twenty-two lots and received the deed; I had but a bond for security of our bargains.[116]

If I had some trouble in securing property for the church, the Right Rev. Bishop had much more trouble to come to the determination of accepting the bishopric of St. Paul. It was but one or two days previous to his consecration that he gave his consent, and I was told by himself, that he would never have done it, had it not been for the Right Rev. Bishop of Belley, Monseigneur Devie, for whom he had always the greatest respect on account of his talents and piety. He exposed to him the state of things in the new diocese of St. Paul, and asked him if he thought he could refuse the charge without sin. The opinion of Monseigneur Devie was, that he was bound, sub gravi, to accept. He then gave his consent and was consecrated on the 26th of January, 1851. 'Omnia omnibus factus sum' was the motto engraved on his seal, and in fact the first bishop of St. Paul, like the Apostle of Nations, was 'all to all.' All those who have been well acquainted with him are convinced that he constantly walked in the footsteps of St. Paul, by zeal, piety, charity, humility, incessant labor and patience in sufferings; not only after his consecration, but also when a priest, when in the seminary, and in the colleges. I was not acquainted with him, it is true, before 1838; but my assertion is founded on the testimony of persons who had been much edified by his conduct even when he was beginning his studies.

The Right Rev. Bishop spent yet three or four months in Europe after his consecration, in order to procure some laborers for the extensive vineyards entrusted to his care,

---

116 Vital Guerin, however, died in poverty, although once having an estimated worth of $150,000. in land, a fortune in those days. A generous man, perhaps he donated or sold too cheaply too many tracts of his property to church and civic organizations. He passed away in 1870.

and many things necessary for the establishment of a new diocese. On the day of the feast of the Visitation of the Blessed Virgin Mary, the 2d of July, 1851, I had the long expected and desired visit of the Right Rev. Bishop, who arrived at St. Paul, accompanied by two priests and three seminarians. To describe the pleasure I felt at their arrival would be a difficult task. I had been for seven years without any brother priest, except a few weeks, during which another clergyman resided with me in St. Paul."[117]

Joseph Cretin continued as bishop for the next five years, dying of what seems to have been congestive heart failure in February of 1857. He was some months short of his 58th year. Cretin was a very successful leader, indeed. At the time of his death there were twenty-nine churches in his diocese, whereas he had started with less than five. The see having become suddenly vacant, Augustin Ravoux was appointed administrator and he saw to it that the first St. Paul cathedral was completed in 1858. After a hiatus of over two years, Thomas Langdon Grace became the second bishop of St. Paul.

Ravoux lived far longer than Bishop Cretin, being 91 years old at his death in 1906 at St. Joseph's Hospital. The following contemporary description is given of the man, for so many years the one remaining link to the inauguration of the Catholic church in Minnesota: *"Very few of our citizens who notice a tall, spare man, with a long, flowing coat and taking extended strides upon our streets, ever wielding a cane in a peculiar manner, now throwing it out from the arm, and then bringing it down upon the pavement as he moves along, would suppose that this was Very Rev. Father Ravoux, who came to St. Paul in 1841, or forty-four years ago; and yet his face is familiar to all the old settlers and his kind voice has been heard in many a lowly hovel. He was*

---

117 Perhaps they somehow missed one another, but Fr. Florimond Bonduel did visit St. Paul, St. Anthony Falls, St. Croix, etc., probably during the summer of 1846. Also, Bishop Loras once again traveled to the area in 1847, accompanied by a Father Donaghoe.

born in France in 1815, and is consequently seventy years old. In 1838 he offered his services to Bishop Loras, of Dubuque, then in Europe, as a missionary in the West, and soon after entered upon his duties, preaching in various parts of the then territory; learning the Sioux language; printing books in the Sioux tongue...Among the books he printed in the Indian language, was one with a very peculiar title, viz: 'Wa-Kan-tan-Ka ti Cancu,' meaning, 'Path to the House of God.' He was well adapted to mingle with the Indians, as he readily learned their language and by his mild and gentle disposition won their regard...

Father Ravoux is a marked character upon the streets, or anywhere else. His dress indicates his calling. With a kind, benevolent face, broad forehead and slender body, he moves along with the aid of his walking stick, with all the agility of a man of forty. He is a strong orthodox upholder of the Catholic Church and believes in the positive punishment of all violators of the law of God; or at least what he honestly thinks to be the law of God. Several years ago he was engaged in arranging some drapery in the church and had his mouth full of pins, when he fell and some of these pins passed down into his wind pipe and some stuck in his throat, and he has suffered more or less from this accident ever since. It has affected his preaching somewhat, but still he has performed great labors in the field and in the church, and is yet a grand, venerable specimen of an old-time Catholic priest."[118]

The name of the priest who visited Ravoux was Lacombe, a Canadian. In 1920, Katherine Hughes published a biography of Father Albert Lacombe,[119] who, in 1849, was scheduled to go to that far-off mission at Pembina on the Red River and join Father Belcourt. Lacombe stopped at Dubuque to confer with Bishop Loras

---

118 Newson, *Pen Pictures of St. Paul, Minnesota, and biographical sketches of old settlers, etc., ibid.*
119 *Father Lacombe: Black-Robe Voyageur*, McClelland and Stewart, [Toronto,1920].

and Father Cretin and was soon on his way upriver to St. Paul.

"For twelve days the boat puffed its slow way up the current, passing occasional encampments of Indians on the green banks. Here in the stillness and free airs of the wilderness the spirit of the great West first came to Father Lacombe. "I began to breathe freely at last; I felt myself a new man," he says of those delightful days on the Mississippi. One day the boatmen called to him that St. Paul was at hand. He hurried forward to look on the scattered settlement of log-houses, whose occupants were hurrying down to the riverside to meet the boat."

Father Ravoux was one of those and brought his young guest to the log chapel built by Galtier in 1841. Hughes mentions that on the same site *"a large newspaper office now stands"*. This was where Albert Lacombe was to stay while he waited for the Red River brigade to arrive.[120]

When Lacombe asked where he was to sleep, Ravoux pointed out a box, saying there were blankets inside. When the Canadian protested that it looked to him like the box was a coffin, Ravoux confirmed the suspicion. A *metis* had died in the woods and the priest had helped to make the coffin, only to discover it was too short for its intended occupant. Another had to be fashioned, but the thrifty Ravoux had decided the first one would do very well for his expected visitor.[121]

Albert Lacombe remained a month with Augustin Ravoux until the train of ox-carts arrived, sent by Father Belcourt to escort him to Pembina. Ravoux was also known to Archbishop John Ireland, who was one of two Irish lads from St. Paul who journeyed with the strait-laced priest to France in order to enter the seminary at Meximieux. Ireland, given to mischief in his youth, hid a bottle of wine in the

---

120 The men sent by Father Georges Belcourt for supplies and to pick up Lacombe.

121 As Hughes claimed to have known Fr. Lacombe personally, he was doubtless the source of the anecdote.

satchel of Ravoux, which broke and saturated the priest's things. That Monsignor Ravoux was, in his own way, a "tough specimen" no one could deny. He is buried in St. Paul's Calvary Cemetery.

CALIFORNIA FOR VIRGINIA

In 1854 a pregnant Virgina Ivins and her husband, William, decided to go to California, taking their son, aged one year. At the eleventh hour, Dr. and Mrs. Galland had made up their minds to accompany them. One suspects that Isaac Galland could simply not pass up the chance at adventure. Ever since the Gold Rush that occurred around the year 1849, there had been a large migration of westward pioneers. Virginia sets the scene of the crossing of the Missouri River that spring: *"On reaching the flat we found, however, that there were at least five hundred wagons before us with thousands of cattle waiting to cross and were told that we must wait our turn, which probably would not come for several days. My husband was in no mood for waiting, so watching his opportunity he rushed in while some slower person was getting ready and before night we were on the Nebraska side and made our camp where the city of Omaha is now situated. To celebrate our fortunate start we killed a fine calf and feasted on the last fresh meat we had for three months, excepting occasionally when some one would kill a jack rabbit or a sage hen, although they were not very plentiful.*

At an early hour on the morning of May second we took up our line of march toward the Golden West on the broad well beaten road, which was lined with vehicles of every description, cattle, horses, sheep and mules with men, women and children walking to save the beasts of burden. We were almost always in sight of trains for the first five hundred miles, further on as the roads branched off leading to different points or passes we were more alone. It was a bright, beautiful morning and our courage was renewed by having made so successful a start west of the Missouri river."

Virginia's little boy, Charley, contracted "lung fever", possibly pneumonia, along the way and Isaac Galland proved he was no quack by curing the tot. Some months later, after his niece's daughter was born in California, the doctor pulled Virginia through some type of delirious fever. After living for three years in Petaluma, Dr. and Mrs. Galland apparently found no reason to stay on and Mr. and Mrs. Ivins, after all the trouble of getting to California, decided to follow them back east. A very long voyage leaving from San Francisco somehow landed the couple and their children at New York.

"September twenty-ninth gave me no thrill of pleasure, for I was already longing for my California home. We remained in quarantine all night; no one went to bed, but sang songs, played cards, danced and tried to while away the weary hours. Some one struck up the song, 'The sun shines bright on my California home,' and I longed for the lonely ranch, even to the coyotes and the grizzly bears. I begged my husband to make a visit and go back, but he said again he never put his hand to the plow and looked back; so with a heavy heart I journeyed on to Keokuk to meet many dear friends who were so kind that after awhile I became reconciled to remain where my lot seemed to be cast, but I have never ceased to remember with pleasure my loved home in the land of sunshine and flowers."

Virginia Ivins died on November 23, 1924 at Keokuk. Her remains are interred in Oakland Cemetery there.

Photo-engraving of Lucien Galtier
toward the end of his life

GALTIER AT ST. GABRIEL'S

A researcher and avid historian named Peter L. Scanlan wrote to Father William Busch of St. Paul about an item of interest to both men. Scanlan, a medical doctor by profession, who had an office above the Prairie du Chien post office, rendered a short description to Fr. Busch of a bound journal of about 340 pages, the diary of the late Father Lucien Galtier.[122] Although Dr. Scanlan later wrote that this journal had become lost sometime previous to 1929,[123] he makes it obvious that its contents had the potential of being very useful to a biographer of the priest, even though Scanlan opined that *"it is of some Historical value but is not of so much as I had hoped it to be from what I had been told."* But the doctor probably underestimated how much even mundane jottings can reveal about an individual's character.

Father Galtier apparently used this journal for his housekeeping accounts, church business, his real estate transactions, and even his activities as an agent, since 1854, for the banking firm of "Fanechon and Gaillard", which ended up going bust sometime after the priest's death. That is what Dr. Scanlan claimed to Fr. Busch, but it is abundantly clear that Auguste Gaillard and Jules

---

122 Letter in Minnesota Historical Society collections.
123 Scanlan, P. L., Dr. "Pioneer Priests at Prairie Du Chien". The Wisconsin Magazine of History December 1929: 97-106. Born, 1862, died 1956. [Update: The author found what appears to be the remnant of the journal in Sept. 2012 at the old rectory of St. Gabriel's church.]

Famechon began a "general stock" store in 1849, built a large stone building on Bluff St., and that Mr. Famechon was still doing business in 1884.[124] Why Scanlan, who knew the history of his town quite well, would mention G&F in connection with a bank is rather odd. Such an enterprise was established in 1856 "by a man from Milwaukee" [Anson Eldred] but, by 1883, the bank had become a vinegar factory! No bank evidently existed as early as 1854 in the village of Prairie du Chien. Nevertheless, it is clear that some of his parishioners preferred that Lucien hold onto their savings for them, even though it seems to us now a strange service for a cleric to render.

One wonders where Galtier boarded from 1847-49 in the days before he had his own housekeepers, but the diary went into detail about that, as well. Since the priest had a wine bill, Scanlan made it his business to investigate Lucien's habits and discovered that the man was a "total abstainer". The wine was apparently for the mass.

Much more interesting than all the accounting is the fact that Father Galtier was a botanist and, as Dr. Scanlan wrote to Busch, *"On the last pages of this book are a large number of plants listed showing...that he took pains to become acquainted with a large number of wild flowers still common to this locality."*

Since only a few pages remain of the diary, one can't write much about the day-to-day life of Lucien Galtier at St. Gabriel's except that, having found a permanent home, he must have kept occupied with his duties and many interests. Just as the church building has changed quite a bit since Galtier's day, so has Prairie du Chien, itself. Many of the structures familiar to the priest have been destroyed by fire, ruined, or moved due to annual flooding, and others demolished in more recent times. Businesses and their

---

[124] From *Historical and Biographical Sketches of Prairie du Chien*, 1884. It seems Scanlan got his facts wrong or perhaps misread a French entry in the diary. Galtier's script can be difficult to decipher and he was probably not an agent for a bank at all.

signs have come and gone, while some of the buildings that housed them still remain, such as that of Famechon on Bluff St. Even the grand Dousman mansion, now known as the Villa Louis, looked different then, although it stood in the same location.

↑ Man with horse-drawn wagon on Bluff Street

Going into the commercial part of town from his house on Church St. [now Beaumont Road] Father Galtier would have seen the Law Block, a brick structure Hercules Dousman had built, which contained the offices of lawyers. Heading down Main St., an old Indian trail, the priest would have passed by the Traner Carriage Works and Kane's Hotel, which stood next to the log house of Antoine Boisvert. That was the Main St. of the mid-19th Century, small residences and larger commercial buildings all together. When a fire started in Boisvert's stable in November of 1872, it soon overcame Kane's Hotel and the carriage works.

Whenever Galtier crossed the bridge over the slough that separated the island of St. Feriole from the rest of Prairie du Chien, he would have seen a number of buildings that still exist today. Joe Rolette had begun work on his frame house but died before it could be finished. Yet finished it, was and now stands near the Dousman House hotel. North of this was the home Rolette had commissioned for his estranged wife, Jane, which she gave to a member of the Brisbois family [into which she had been adopted] not long after. There was the Brisbois store, also made of stone, and other establishments and homes of wood. A log cabin, built by Charles Erdenberger in 1859, still survives. Also in later years, there was the railroad depot, now a bar with plenty of old-time atmosphere.

There were still soldiers at Fort Crawford when Galtier first arrived at Prairie du Chien, and the garrison was occupied until 1856. During the Civil War, the fort was used as a hospital and saw plenty of activity. After that the buildings slowly fell into ruin, although the large residence of the commanding officer held up far longer. One commander, future US president Zachary Taylor, had lived there. Eventually, Protestants had erected their own churches in Prairie du Chien and, very near St. Gabriel's, was the long, frame house occupied, it is said, by its earliest pastors.[125]

Unfortunately, the archdiocese of Milwaukee claims to possess only one letter written by Father Galtier to Bishop Henni. Therefore, lacking the journal, it is not possible for us to know much about the thoughts or state of mind of the pastor, which would not be reflected in the brief entries of baptisms,[126] weddings, and funerals, the other records kept by the priest. These old records of St. Gabriel's have been transferred to the La Crosse diocese archives. Once the diocese of La Crosse was created, Prairie du Chien would have fallen within its jurisdiction, being not many miles south of this episcopal see. Michael Heiss, the superior of St. Francis Seminary at Milwaukee, was named the first bishop but, as the diocese was not established by Pope Pius IX until March of 1868, Galtier never served under him.

Far from remaining comfortably at his rectory, Father

---

125 Built by Pierre LaRiviere, it became known as the LaRiviere-Ravoux house.
126 1,762 individuals, according to one source.

Galtier proved he retained the pioneer spirit by making himself useful wherever he could in the outlying missions and—yes—constructing more log houses of worship. At some point it had probably registered in Lucien's mind that being associated with the "dirty work of a carpenter" brought him closer to another such one who had lived centuries before. While still at Keokuk, Galtier had written to Bishop Loras that he knew his abilities and inclinations better than he had before, believed he was better suited to the Old World, but the passage of time would prove him wrong in his self-assessment.

He built St. Mark's chapel at the Kickapoo mission [mentioned in the letter of Father Bonduel] in 1855. La Crosse being one of the missions attended by the pastor of St. Gabriel's, Galtier erected its first log church in that same busy year, although he had first gone to the settlement in 1851. In fact, La Crosse remained a mission of the priest until 1860.

Between 1853 and 1856 Father Galtier visited St. John the Baptist mission at Mifflin, Iowa County, once per month. Another chapel was constructed under his supervision at Utica, Crawford County, in 1855. That very same year the tireless priest built the log church at Mt. Hope and on Irish Ridge he obtained a plot of forty acres to be used for church purposes. In 1856 Galtier traveled to Boyd, another mission of Crawford County. and a year later a church was erected there called St. Philip's. And so on it went. It happened that a place called Boscobel was on the eastern limit of the Milwaukee diocese. Father Galtier first visited the site in 1859 and offered masses there on many occasions. Muscoda, Liberty, Bee Town, Waterloo, Georgetown, and DeSoto all saw the ministry of this devoted man. Closer to home, there was the mission called Pigeon and a few others, in addition.

Regarding pigeons, Albert Coryer [Carriere], born in Prairie du Chien in 1877, wrote down some unpublished stories he had heard from his parents and grandparents about pioneer life in the area. One of them had to do with the wild pigeons, which were extremely plentiful and a ready food source until the prairie had been given over to farming. Then they became a nuisance and a threat to the production of grain. Sometimes the birds darkened the sky for hours. According to Coryer, in the early 1860's the pastors of the Catholic churches of the Mississippi Valley arranged to make a novena to exile the wild pigeons for 99 years. Not long afterward the pigeons became extinct but not before migrating to the eastern seacoast and vainly trying to fly across the Atlantic. If Father Galtier had any part in this praying for a miracle, it is not evident.

During the nineteen years that Galtier was based at Prairie du Chien, he seems to have taken a few leaves of absence. Father Antoine Godfert substituted for him in 1850, Galtier likely having left to make his bid for donations at New Orleans. According to John Ireland, Lucien made those visits to St. Paul in 1853 and 1865. In 1857 Jean Claude Perrodin took over while Galtier was away on a trip to Europe. There may have been other visits to Europe of which the author is not aware.

Back in 1849 Father Galtier was shocked to learn that Louis Maynard had been killed by Theophilus La Chappelle and his house burned down, as well. La Chappelle was found not guilty by reason of insanity. On May 2nd of that same year a paper called *The Patriot* published the following ad: *"A New School. We rejoice to announce to our friends that a Catholic Female School to be conducted by Miss P. McLeod under the patronage and inspection of the Rev. L. Galtier will commence on the 15th of this month. The discipline will be mild but strict; cleanliness is particularly desired. Reading, writing, arithmetic, English grammar, history, geography, plain sewing, marking and needle work will be equally taught to children according to their capacity. Terms will be moderate. Previous application for admission should be made immediately to either the Rev. L. Galtier or to Miss McLeod."*

There can be no doubt Father Galtier was anxious to provide some education for the Catholic girls of the town in order to broaden their horizons. Born in Scotland in 1815, Penelope McLeod was certainly a member of the priest's congregation, but her qualifications for conducting the teaching of the girls are not known. Suffice it to say that Miss McLeod must have acquired some education and had the confidence of Galtier. It will shortly become apparent that she retained his good opinion for the rest of his life and that they were probably friends.

In May of 1859, a decade later, the town experienced one of its worst floods ever. Prairie du Chien, in the meantime, had undergone many changes. The town's newspaper, the *Courier* [still existing as the *Courier Press*], printed the following on January 8, 1857: *"A line of steamers is building, to run in connection with the railroad from Prairie du Chien to St. Paul; that during the past year, two new brick hotels have been completed, and two others remodeled; two steam ferry boats, to cross the river to McGregor, have been purchased; one new church, erected; three splendid brick blocks, nineteen stores, two breweries, one steam flouring mill, and about a hundred dwelling houses put up, besides the extensive works of the railroad company. Five brick yards, two stone quarries, three lumber yards and one saw-mill have been inadequate to meet the demands required for improvements."*

On January 22, 1866 Father Galtier wrote a longish letter to Bishop Henni in very nearly perfect English. Among other things, he mentions a visit he had made to Rome, during which he had advocated for the establishment of a new diocese in western Wisconsin. Ten years later, this was still on his mind. He told Henni that it might be a good plan to divide the state in half, *"east and west as it is naturally by the River Wisconsin."* It may have been that Galtier was contemplating another journey to Rome, because he wrote:

"I do think to obtain this great favor [the bishopric] for anyone named—provided I receive a letter of introduction to his eminence Cardinal Barnabo from Your Lordship together with your consent of dividing [the diocese]...in this I have no self interest, it is for merely the glory of God...I could say much more on this important matter which now is pending since 1857 or more but this is enough."[127]

The avowal of a lack of self-interest may have been completely true. We have no real idea of the state of Father Galtier's health at this time, although he was apparently optimistic that he could manage a long voyage. Yet Galtier was only human and, being past fifty, he may have felt he had sufficient experience to become a bishop and that there was no one with more seniority in all of western Wisconsin. Nor had the priest been previously overlooked when it came to a higher office. In 1855 when Prairie du Chien had been proposed for a new episcopal see, the suggested candidates for its bishop had been Father Henry Juncker of the Cincinnati diocese; Father Lucien Galtier of Milwaukee and Father Antoine Pelamourgues, vicar general of Dubuque. When the elevation of Prairie du Chien was dropped, Galtier was short-listed for a diocese to be created in Nebraska but then his nomination and that of Father Pelamourgues were switched for St. Paul in 1857. Due to the passing of Bishop Cretin, there had been a vacancy, not quickly filled.

In this same letter to Henni, the pastor [and now a vicar general of Milwaukee] writes on behalf of his nephew, Louis [?] Galtier, residing in St. Affrique,[128] who was evidently also a priest and desired nothing but to come to America. Galtier had learned that "father Decailli of Keokuk", grandnephew of Mathias Loras, was in France and

---

127 University of Notre Dame Archives., New Orleans.
128 The same place Galtier was born. In Galtier's will, the nephew is called "Lucien", apparently also a priest. Galtier may have had two nephews in the priesthood but can have miswritten the first name in one instance. Both documents in which a nephew is mentioned were written on January 22.

thought that his own nephew could cross the Atlantic with him. Louis De Cailly was well-known to Father Galtier as, during every month of the year 1856, the younger man had traveled a distance of about sixty miles from Fort Atkinson, Iowa, to confess to him. Born in Lyons in 1832, Fr. De Cailly came to America in 1847 to labor in the Iowa missions. He was not ordained until 1854, however. Bishop Loras was tough on his relative and the young man spent ten years in Keokuk. Still, even he left the diocese in 1868 to join that of Columbus, Ohio. By then, of course, Mathias Loras was dead. Yet De Cailly came back to Iowa in 1884 to serve at Davenport and after that he was at Fort Madison for fourteen years. Evidently a much-loved man, being liberal and broad-minded, De Cailly wrote a biography of Loras and was soon after killed in a tragic accident. Driving his buggy from Keokuk to his home in Fort Madison, the priest died instantly when hit by a train. This was on July 11, 1898.

    Galtier had the money for his nephew's passage, but complained to Bishop Henni that a local banker wanted too much to convert it into funds that the nephew could use. Therefore, Galtier proposed that the *"gentlemen of the propagation"* at Lyons pay one thousand francs to the younger Galtier and that he, himself, would refund the exact same amount to Henni at any time. Lucien Galtier, at this point in his life, was by no means a poor man. He appears even to have owned his own home.

    That same day, either before or after writing to Bishop Henni, Lucien Galtier drafted his will. One wonders why he didn't do it sooner, as human life in the 19th Century hung by a tenuous thread and it was not unknown for entire families to be wiped out by evils the nature of which were poorly comprehended by most. One of these was Black Measles or hemorrhagic measles, a rare but highly contagious illness that proved the horrible fate of the Kimmel family, living not far from Prairie du Chien, just the previous year. Nineteen-year-old John Kimmel, a Civil War soldier, had perished of the Black Measles and his body was sent home. His parents, understandably wanting to see their son one last time, made the mistake of opening his coffin. Within days, the father and five remaining Kimmel children, including a baby, succumbed to the disease. The devastated mother survived to bury her husband and half of her offspring in the Crow Hollow Cemetery of Crawford County.

On the other hand, persons of the area sometimes reached a remarkable old age, such as Antoine Valley, who died in Prairie du Chien on Feb. 28, 1881 in his 104th year. Valley settled there in 1854 and was the father of eighteen children, nine of whom survived him. The secret of his longevity was reputed to have been a total abstinence from alcoholic beverages. Another gentleman, Louis St. Jacque, died on Dec. 28, 1945 at that age of 93. He now rests in the graveyard behind St. Gabriel's church but, a few years prior to his passing, St. Jacque had something to say about the last time he saw Father Lucien Galtier alive.

"Ma chandelle est morte; je n'ai plus de feu..."[129]

THE FINAL DAYS OF GALTIER

The view of St. Gabriel's sanctuary, below, is not quite the one Lucien Galtier saw. A number of changes had been made, but the interior is still very reminiscent of what it had been prior to 1866.

Interior of St. Gabriel's ca. 1900[130]

Today, Galtier would scarcely know his own church could he see it, it is so much altered both inside and out. The exterior is more ornate and the interior far more

---
129 Lyrics from an old French song, "Au Clair de la Lune", dating back to the mid 18th century. "My candle is dead; I have no more fire".
130 Wisconsin Historical Society, image #42040

austere, yet St. Gabriel's remains a beautiful landmark that fairly exudes history along with about 170 years worth of incense. The place smells absolutely divine.

If Father Galtier had made any sort of personal plans in the winter of 1866, a very poignant document[131] demonstrates their futility and how suddenly his life was extinguished. Since fall the priest had been officiating at one funeral a month, at least. He buried two persons in September, including a girl of sixteen months. The parish saw another death in October and three more in November, two of them being children. A young man aged 20-22 by Father Galtier's reckoning passed away in January. All these notations are in the St. Gabriel's register, written in Galtier's fine penmanship. His last entry is: *"On the second of February, A.D., 1866, I buried in the Catholic Cemetery the corp. of Michael Dignan, who died on the 21st of last january in faith whereof..."* Why it took so long for poor Michael to be interred cannot be known. Perhaps the ground was too frozen at the time of death. However, the next entry is not in Father Galtier's hand.

"On the 25th of february A.D. 1866 I have buried the V. R. Father L. Galtier pastor of St. Gabriels Church who died on the 21st instant. R. in Pace, J. C. Perrodin."

This was Father Jean Claude Perrodin, who should have been stationed at *Fond du Lac, Wisconsin, then, a distance of at least 120 miles from Prairie du Chien.*[132] What he recorded was undisputed fact, but the circumstances surrounding the death of Galtier are rather mysterious and accompanied by contradictions.

A Jesuit named Father August Siebauer, attached to Campion Catholic High School for boys at Prairie du Chien,

---

131 Courtesy of the diocese of La Crosse.
132 Although Louis St. Jacque had evidently claimed that Fr. Perrodin was at Maquoketa, Iowa. This priest had not been with the Iowa missions since 1851, however. Perhaps he had been visiting his former parish.

also wrote a letter to Father William Busch[133] of St. Paul. It bears the date of October 25, 1955. Father Siebauer had taken the trouble to interview Louis St. Jacque, who had, so many years before, been an altar boy of Lucien Galtier from 1863 to 1866. St. Jacque was ninety at the time of the interview, which took place more than a decade earlier.

Entry by Fr. Perrodin of the burial of Fr. Galtier

---

133 1882-1971. Professor of Church History at the St. Paul Seminary.

Louis St. Jacque, born in 1852 in Quebec, was eleven years old when Father Galtier approached him about serving mass on weekdays. According to Louis, these masses were not said in the St. Gabriel's church building but in the chapel of "the long frame house" to which description the LaRiviere-Ravoux house at 316 No. Beaumont Road fits.

House where Fr. Galtier may have said his last mass

Although this structure had purportedly housed Augustin Ravoux and Joseph Cretin years before, Lucien Galtier did not live there in 1866 but in a red brick house across the street from St. Gabriel's, which has since been demolished. It is not clear which house was meant.

The priest had cautioned young Louis that he needed someone reliable. If the boy thought he could manage to get there early every morning, Galtier would buy him a new suit of clothes and a pair of boots. This is what Louis received by way of incentive and the lad did prove that he could be relied upon. He was the eldest male child of the twelve offspring his parents, Toussaint and Julia, produced.

Three years passed and Louis St. Jacque was going to be fourteen on the 4th of July. However, on the morning of February 20 it was Father Galtier who was late. When he did arrive, Louis noticed that he was holding a blood-stained handkerchief to his chin. The boy asked the priest what had happened and Galtier replied that he had cut himself while shaving and could not get the bleeding to stop. Galtier vested and said mass, but the bleeding continued and the pastor had to pause a few times to deal with it.

Louis St. Jacque[134]

Louis tidied up after mass and saw that Father Galtier was seated on a chair, his head in his hands. He appeared pale and very tired. When the altar boy expressed concern, Lucien told him that he felt absolutely exhausted. St. Jacque said that he then helped the priest "to his room", which was probably in that house across the way. Galtier assured the boy that he would feel better after a rest and some breakfast and so Louis, not suspecting anything

---

134 Courtesy of Phil Gokey [Gauthier] grand-nephew of Louis St. Jacque.

serious, went home. Decades later, he had evidently told Father Siebauer that *"it was not possible to find out what befell Father Galtier during the day"* and whatever else Louis knew he had obtained second hand. Apparently Peter Scanlan also interviewed the elderly St. Jacque, who allowed that *"One report had it that he heard some confessions in the afternoon."*[135]

This, then, is what has been generally believed ever since about the last day of the life of Lucien Galtier at Prairie du Chien, even though its origin is what a man of ninety recalled about a day in February when he was thirteen. Still, traumatic experiences tend to leave a lasting impression on the memory and it doubtless shocked Louis that a person he had seen so often for nearly three years could disappear forever so abruptly. To the boy it must have seemed a death without warning and so it was recalled.

In 1986 St. Gabriel's celebrated its sesquicentennial of existence. In commemoration, a committee printed a history of the parish on what seems to have been a calendar. It mentions, in addition to pointing out Lucien's talents as an artist, singer, and violinist, *"Father Galtier died an untimely death in 1866 when he accidentally cut a carbuncle while shaving. He contracted blood poisoning and died the next day—February 21, 1866. Father's home was willed to the Dominican sisters to be used as a school for French children."*

However, tangible contemporary evidence tells a different tale. It may be very true that Father Galtier had cut himself while shaving on the 20th and that he was having difficulty stanching the flow of blood. The sight of bleeding makes one take notice but young Louis St. Jacque may not have been so aware [or did not remember] that his parish priest had been ailing for days. Galtier might have been coughing—was probably exhibiting signs of a respiratory inflammation—but it was, after all, still winter and a cold

---
135 From a slightly different version than that of Fr. Siebauer, attributed to Dr. Scanlan. Courtesy of the St. Paul Cathedral archives.

nothing remarkable.

Nor was it so very unusual for a man to die during the 19th Century merely because he had nicked his face with a razor if a carbuncle was involved. A carbuncle [which the French called "anthrax"] is a collection of boils and is full of *staphylococcus aureus* bacteria or a form of *streptococcus*. Before the advent of antibiotics, a cut could facilitate the poison entering the blood stream, causing a state of septicemia, which could prove fatal. The blood around the cut stagnates and forms a culture medium where the bacteria already present increases some forty times in potency if the wound is not properly disinfected.

However, it was possible for the body to fight off the septicemia. In his paper in the American Journal of the Medical Sciences, Vol. 80 [1880], *Carbuncle of the Face,* F. A. Burrall M.D. described his careful treatment of a young man of twenty, whose temperature rose to 105 during his bout with the sepsis, caused by a carbuncle near the lip, over some days— but who survived. Among the substances used to treat him were Peruvian balsam, carbolic acid, tincture of iodine to paint the throat, which also became infected, muriate of iron, and oiled silk for a dressing upon the carbuncle, itself. But Burrall made it clear that a carbuncle of the face, nicked or not, was a very grave matter as *"The serious element of the disease appears to be a tendancy to septicaemia as the result of absorbtion."* Moreover, many 19th Century physicians believed these carbuncles were symptomatic of a "broken down constitution" and that persons suffering from diabetes were especially susceptible to the infection.

To give the reader an idea of the course of the illness, Dr. Burrall first saw the young man on Jan. 28, yet the patient had already not been feeling well for a few days. He had a temperature of 100 and *"there were one or two acne-like pustules near the left corner of the mouth"*. By the second day of his treatment, the physician noted that the swelling of the face had increased. On the third day

Burrall incised the swelling and found it carbuncular. By now the patient's fever had risen to 104½. The 31st of January had Dr. Burrall indicating the patient had spent a restless night and was experiencing diarrhea. His pulse and temperature remained very high. The young man only began to improve on Feb. 4th but began showing signs of respiratory problems, spitting up bloody froth. By Feb. 12th the doctor recorded that the sick man *"has improved steadily"*. He was taking porter and cod liver oil for strength in addition to the tincture muriate of iron. On Mar. 12, an entire month later, the patient was still ill but continued to be on the mend.

It may be that Dr. Burrall's carbuncular case only survived his ordeal because he was twenty [although the physician stated he seemed "delicate"], but in the spring of 1923, a British peer of the realm, Lord Carnarvon, the wealthy sponsor of the excavation of the tomb of the pharaoh Tutankhamun, happened to nick an infected mosquito bite while shaving. Carnarvon, age fifty-seven, had been in frail health for some time and had been advised to spend his winters away from the English damp—in this case Egypt. On March 17th, the earl was diagnosed with erysipelas and streptococcic blood poisoning, but did not succumb to the ensuing complication of pneumonia until the 5th of April.

A famous individual, who died as a result of carbuncle of the face and whose demise has been well described, was Russian pianist and composer, Alexander Scriabin, 1871-1915.[136] On the 4th of April, the musician noticed a small pimple on his upper right lip. This lesion changed from a carbuncle into a single boil in appearance but its color was described as "purple fire", which spread. By April 7 Scriabin was in bed and his fever actually rose to 106 on the 10th and remained at this level all day. An incision was made into the swollen face with no pus

---
136 Bowers, Faubion, *Scriabin, a Biography: Second, Revised Edition,* Dover Publications [2011]

resulting but a test of the blood showed both strep and staph. On April 12 the doctors had not yet pronounced Scriabin's case a hopeless one and the pianist even seemed to improve a little, the swelling of the face went down, but he soon got an agonizing pain in his chest. Pleurisy was deemed the cause and it was becoming apparent that blood poisoning had tainted Scriabin's entire system and he was doomed. However, the diagnosis of pleurisy may have been in error. The patient grew increasingly short of breath and delirious. He died on April 15.

Yet, according to Louis St. Jacque, Father Galtier, a person of fifty-four, cut himself while shaving before morning mass, seemed weak, and then suddenly lapsed into a coma at midnight, dying at about three or four in the morning of the next day. Due to the challenges connected with carbuncle of the face [or elsewhere on the body] doctors of the 19th and early 20th Centuries often described their encounters with the malady in the literature but, in her research, the present writer has not come across a single instance where the afflicted succumbed within the space of one day or less than 48 hours after first being seen by the physician. Nor, assuming that Father Galtier already had a lesion on his chin for several days [as must have been the case], has she found examples of where the individual was still up and about so shortly prior to expiring—except one and that is merely from an obituary with scant details.[137]

---

[137] " *Mr. James L. McPhail, well known in Baltimore and Washington in connection with the government detective service, died suddenly at his residence... early yesterday morning. Mr. McPhail was a special agent of the Postoffice Department, and has been suffering for some weeks from a carbuncle on the chin. On Thursday of last week he visited Washington on official duty, and attended to business up to Monday evening. After retiring on Monday night he was seized with sudden illness about midnight, and his physician was summoned, but he expired in a few hours. Mr. McPhail was in his fifty-ninth year...*" Baltimore Sun, Oct. 6, 1874. Here, however, we have no doctor to attest that McPhail's carbuncle was the direct cause of his death—although it was obviously suspected as the culprit by someone.

Judging by the case histories of those days before antibiotics could come to the rescue, Galtier's chin ought to have pained him greatly by the 20th of February with his face not only bleeding from the cut but the discoloration and swelling already so pronounced that St. Jacque would have been appalled by it.

A carbuncle whose malignancy had reached a near-fatal point *should* also have occasioned a high fever on the 20th, so that the priest would have been in no condition to shave at all, much less stand on his feet long enough to say mass—if he was going to die of blood poisoning within the next 24 hours.

Thirteen-year-old Louis may have been convinced that something Lucien Galtier had nicked on his chin, which bled so profusely, had killed him. But some papers that belong to the probate of the will of the deceased do not indicate a man merely having a mishap on the morning of the 20th of February and consequently expiring in the early hours of the 21st.

A Dr. Smyth of McGregor, Iowa, directly across the Mississippi from Prairie du Chien, submitted an account to the probate court, asking to be reimbursed for visits to Father Galtier's house on the 18th and and 19th days of February. The physician's bill amounts to all of ten dollars and indicates no subsequent attendance.[138]

The bill of J. Tilmont, druggist, shows that, on February 18th, "Spanish fly plasters", used for raising a blister to draw out an inflammation, were purchased by or for Father Galtier. The plasters were employed in the treatment of respiratory ailments and others, as well. The idea was to apply the plasters as soon as possible when various illnesses were suspected and to leave them on for twelve hours in the case of an adult.

In fact, Dr. L. W. Pritchard wrote in *The Medical*

---

[138] However, that does not mean a Prairie du Chien physician was not called in later, one who did not submit a statement to the court.

Standard:[139] *"When called upon to see a case of pneumonia or pleurisy, the first thing I do is to locate its extent and severity, and after so doing, apply to the front side of the chest a Spanish fly plaster, so as to cover from one-third to one-fourth of the diseased lung or pleura, being sure to apply it over the most inflamed part. My experience in over twenty years of active practice has been that with the judicious use of blisters in the treatment of pneumonia and pleurisy, every uncomplicated case can be aborted and its activity terminated in five to ten days. As a counter-irritant, I prefer Spanish fly to mustard."*

Additionally, "Sugar of Lead" and "hops salt" were placed on Galtier's account by Tilmont on that day. The former, *saccharum saturni*, is lead acetate. It was once prescribed for intestinal troubles and, if taken in sufficient quantity over a period, could result in acute lead poisoning. What "hops salt" was intended for is not very clear to the author, except that hops were deemed beneficial to the stomach in addition to having sedative properties.

The accounting of the dry goods store, opened by Gaillard and Famechon[140], shows that, even on the 17th, the things thought necessary for the treatment of a lung ailment were already being bought. One bottle of Madeira wine, 2 yards of flannel and a half pint of alcohol makes it plain that a mustard plaster and even the application of heated shot glasses to the back were planned,[141] as well as a bracing drink. Madeira and porter were much used at the time for aiding weakened constitutions. The flannel was for the mustard poultice.

---

139 Vol. XXII, 1899, page 342.
140 Auguste Gaillard and Jules Famechon. Their establishment was also known as "The French Store" although, in 1866, only J. Famechon remained alive.
141 Known as "cupping". One held a small ball of cotton saturated with rubbing alcohol in a pair of large tweezers and ignited it. Then one heated the inside of a small cup or glass and extinguished the flame. The vessel attached itself firmly to the skin and supposedly drew out inflammation.

By the 19th of February one had run out of mustard and a half pound was purchased at the same establishment in addition to another half pint of alcohol. Whether Dr. Smyth had decided to switch to mustard and cupping or Galtier, himself, simply decided to fall back on these old remedies is uncertain. After all, one did not need a prescription to purchase the ingredients. One pound of prunes and a bottle of "Rhein wine" from Famechon on the 20th indicates more intestinal difficulty and a "light wine" was considered efficacious for the lowering of body temperature. It was also prescribed as an ingredient in a draught called "white wine whey" for a pneumonia patient who ought to refrain from eating while feverish.[142] There was nothing more bought of Tilmont until "Essence of Rose" on the 21st, probably an item related to preparing the body of the unfortunate Galtier for his wake.

From the evidence submitted by the physician and the shopkeepers by virtue of their invoices, one can infer that Lucien Galtier contemplated or began treatment for a lung inflammation with the help of a friend on Saturday the 17th. Dr. Smyth[143] was summoned on Sunday and returned on Monday. Tilmont the Belgian druggist supplied some items on Sunday, whether his store was normally open that day or not. Lucien Galtier must have felt better instead of worse on Tuesday the 20th, as the physician was not sent for again and the priest rose early that day for the purpose of saying mass, according to his altar boy. He may have cut himself that morning while shaving, but this act alone would not have made Father Galtier feel so debilitated that he had

---

142 From "On Pneumonia", a lecture delivered by James Barr, MD at University College, Liverpool, in March of 1900 and printed in the British Medical Journal. "sack whey" or "wine whey" was made from skimmed milk and white wine in equal parts. One poured boiling water over the mixture, let it stand a little, and the curd gathered in a lump and settled to the bottom. A bit of sugar was added and, if possible, a sprig of balm or a slice of lemon.

143 His first name remains unknown at this writing. Why he was called in when there were physicians in Prairie du Chien cannot be known, either.

to be helped to his house after mass by Louis St. Jacque. Nothing appears to have been purchased from either Tilmont or the French Store for the treatment of a carbuncle on the face.

What may have occurred is that Galtier, suffering from a degree of pneumonia and believing he was better because his fever had temporarily subsided, got out of bed when he ought to have remained there. Lucien may have persuaded himself that all he had was a cold or bronchitis, even though it is obvious that Dr. Smyth had diagnosed a worse respiratory problem and was doing all he could about it in 1866. But there is testimony from Louis that the "purple fire" manifested itself, too, because *"his chin and lower lip turned purple, then the upper lip and the face"* by evening. Apparently, Father Galtier had more than one illness troubling him and some of them were potentially fatal.

While still feeling weak, the priest went about his duties, exposing himself to the chilly weather and a chapel that may have been insufficiently heated. This probably worsened the congested state of his lungs by evening, but neither that nor the facial sepsis should have killed Galtier so swiftly. He may have suffered a heart attack in his weakened, febrile, and suffering state, being of an age where such things occur. [If the priest's face had turned purple, the venous stagnation causing it must have resulted in terrible pain.] Or, as probably happened to Alexander Scriabin and others who contracted carbuncle in the middle of the face, staphylococcus sepsis brought on one or more septic infarcts of the lung [blood clots]. Something must have shortened the course of his combined illnesses and at least his agony was not prolonged as, given the circumstances, Galtier's chance of survival was not very good.

Louis St. Jacque grew up to become a bricklayer and stone mason. He and his spouse, Rosina, eventually had twelve children, themselves, which was nothing extraordinary for Roman Catholic families of the time. Louis rests in the St. Gabriel's churchyard with Rosina, his parents, and other members of the St. Jacque family.

The will of Father Lucien Galtier consists of three hand-written pages. The first page, dated January 22, 1866, is in the priest's own hand and likewise the second. The language is English, used for legal matters, even though French was routinely spoken by all those of that background in the Prairie du Chien of the time, a situation that persisted into the 1950's. It was only then that the younger generation began to abandon French. It is interesting to contemplate that, around the time of WW II, there were still a few old people in town [like Louis St. Jacque] who recalled Father Galtier from when they were young or at very least knew they had been baptized by him. Some of their names were Louis Cherrier [1858-1937]; Louis LaBonne [1839-1933]; Alice LaRiviere [1847-1942]; Desire DuCharme [1858-1952]--and they were not the only ones. They were precisely the individuals Dr. Peter Scanlan had in mind when he advised Father William Busch to send a French-speaking person to Prairie du Chien if he wanted interviews from those who had seen Lucien Galtier in the flesh. Meanwhile, another person who would gain fame had been born in either Prairie du Chien or neighboring Eastman in 1903, a little girl named Violet Rose. She is all but forgotten now, having left the area while still a youngster, but she achieved Hollywood stardom on the silent screen under the name of Barbara Bedford.[144]

In the first two pages of the will Galtier mentions some family members and what he intended to donate to them. At the bottom of page two the priest squeezed in the instructions that his coffin was to be "common" and that he should be buried in his "black vestment". The interment was to be "near the front of the church, outside" and there

---

144 Also known as Violet Spencer, her married name. She died in 1981 and is buried in Jacksonville, FL.

ought to be no inscription except "Please Pray for a Sinner".

The third page of the testament is written in a much larger, very different handwriting. Someone else wrote down for Lucien Galtier his wish to appoint, H.L. Dousman, John Lawler, and Barnaby Dunn as the executors. These were prominent men of the town. Galtier attests to this and "I have hereunto set my hand seal this 21st Day of February A. D. 1866" with his now somewhat shaky but wholly recognizable signature. It was the last time the priest would write his name and the original piece of paper upon which he had done it is quite an affecting item. It takes no great feat of imagination to envision the circumstances of the signing and the brave and resigned effort of the dying man to put his affairs in legal order while there was still time. One might even imagine that a painting owned by Father Galtier called "The Death of Louis XIII" hung in the very same room.[145] The king of France had St. Vincent de Paul with him at the end, but Lucien had no one to administer the last rites, give him absolution. He was the only Catholic priest in town.

Jules Famechon, the emporium proprietor, was one of the three witnesses to the signing. In other words, after midnight of the 21st the priest was still capable of writing his name with its usual flourish. It may be that he fell into a comatose state later—he surely realized he was dying—but the exact hour or cause of his passing is not recorded in Crawford County in the form of a death certificate because these were not mandatory in 1866. At any rate, the three witnesses to the signing of the Last Will and Testament also put their signatures to an instrument, intended for the probate court, swearing to the fact that Father Galtier was of "sound disposing mind, memory and understanding, and was under no restraint" on the day of his death, February 21st, when he finally legalized the will he had begun a month earlier.

---

145 The picture, among others, was listed in the inventory of the estate.

Galtier knew that his will was not a negligible matter as it turns out that he had an estate valued at about $12,000. dollars. Since Lucien was a diocesan priest and not in a religious order, he did not take a vow of poverty and had managed to save up a considerable sum for the era. Even the house he lived in and the lot upon which it stood belonged to him. This property he intended to be used for a school and it was willed to the bishop of the Milwaukee Diocese along with a painting of William Tell.[146] Land that Galtier owned in France was bequeathed to his surviving brothers and any cash was to be sent to his sister, Amelie Galtier, in St. Affrique. Lucien requested of his sister that some francs were to be distributed to the poor and that 365 masses should be said "for the rest of my soul". Some vestments and other items were to go to another priest, a nephew, also named Lucien Galtier.

Penelope McLeod

Evidently Galtier had verbally specified that things that did not go directly to St. Gabriel's or the diocese were to be placed for safekeeping in the hands of his most trusted female friend in Prairie du Chien, Miss Penelope McLeod,

---
146 Bishop Henni was born in Switzerland.

the lady from Scotland near his own age, who had no claim to beauty but seems to have been capable and industrious.

Exactly what she was doing with her life in 1866 or for the past twenty years is not clear but, by 1872, Penelope became the companion to the elderly and infirm Jane Dousman. Louis and Nina Dousman having moved away from Prairie du Chien, the mansion was left to the occupancy of Louis's mother until her death in 1882. The younger Dousmans then returned to the villa with their children, whereupon Penelope McLeod assumed the position of housekeeper.

However, to Miss McLeod, herself, Father Galtier left nothing, not even his silver watch, even though he willed some home furnishings to his own current housekeeper, Mary Garvey. Perhaps the two friends, who had known one another since the early days of Galtier's time at St. Gabriel's, agreed that any provision for Miss McLeod might cause too much speculation about the nature of their relationship. Penelope died in 1896 at the age of eighty and is buried in the Dousman family plot in the local Calvary Cemetery.

Father Galtier's funeral expenses were also deducted from his estate. The service was held on Sunday, February 25th. There was $75. for a coffin and $10.50 for a "frame catafalque" of a simple design, which may have included a canopy. The French Store dispensed yards of various black cloth and ribbon for draping the catafalque and a number of candles. J. Tilmont dunned for "disinfecting solution of soda", other disinfectants, including "Chloride of Lime", plus more essential oils. There is so much disinfectant sold by Tilmont and charged to the estate that it is obvious the danger of catching something from a corpse and his surroundings was considerably feared by those close to Galtier in 1866. Some new slippers, a pair of drawers, and silk hose were purchased of Famechon, presumably for the arraying of the deceased.

An altar-type tomb of white marble cost $800. and,

while "Please Pray for a Sinner" was engraved upon its lid,[147] no one had the heart to omit the name of Lucien Galtier, the beginning and ending dates of his life, and the land of his birth. The Latin words for "Rest In Peace" are also to be seen upon the tomb to this very day but have grown quite faint due to the relentless erosion of time and the elements.

Lucien Galtier had managed to live long enough to see the blessed end of the bloody war between the states. In three months time, one of the priest's former flock at Mendota, Amable Turpin, would pass from life at the age of one hundred. Two years after the death of Galtier, the diocese of La Crosse came into being, just as he had envisioned it would.

In his time, St. Gabriel's had become a fully-equipped church, with Stations of the Cross installed in 1858. Just the year previous, the railroad had come to Prairie du Chien, initiating a boom of the town. On the downside, since 1785 there have been at least forty major floods in the area, but Prairie du Chien remains a beautiful, engaging tourist spot with numerous places of historic interest. Major changes to St. Gabriel's were already made in the early 20th Century. In 1908 Father Peter Becker erected the present towers and did some remodeling to the interior in addition. A new rectory was built in 1874[148] and the Franciscan sisters, succeeded by the nuns of Notre Dame, taught at the school. Calvary Cemetery took the place of the old French cemetery blessed by Father Joseph Dunand, a Trappist who organized the Catholics of Prairie du Chien in 1817—long before there ever was a church.

Galtier remained *"un beau"* until he faced his final ordeal. Although what seems to be his last extant

---

147 The tomb can be seen in front of St. Gabriel's on North Beaumont Road,

148 The large house still stands but is no longer used as a home for priests. The parishes of Prairie du Chien are served by one priest and an occasional assistant and one Catholic school suffices for all.

photograph[149] shows a man with hair considerably graying, he is still very handsome with rather innocent eyes. The image below is just a fanciful portrait by an artist based on that photo but it might capture something of the more youthful appearance that charmed Virginia Wilcox.

I would like Thomas Newson to have the last word on the subject of this work: *"Those who knew him speak of him as a man of great decision of character, with a rather strong cast of countenance, large mouth and overshadowing eyebrows. His head sat upon his shoulders like a military chieftain, and he was well chosen to mould and control a heterogeneous mass of men whose lives had been spent almost exclusively upon the frontier. He was a well proportioned man, with a fixed determination to accomplish what he undertook, and he succeeded. Years have fled, changes have been made, the first little, crude log church and the first honest, self-sacrificing priest have passed away, but both will ever live in history made doubly dear by the noble achievements of Rev. Lucian Galtier."*[150]

---

149 It is possibly his only one [the others appear to be artistic renderings based on it] and only an engraving made from it remains. There was a time when photographs could not be reproduced in newspapers and books so the etching process of the likeness was used. The photo is in private hands.

150 Newson, Thomas McClean, *Pen Pictures of St. Paul, Minnesota, and Biographical Sketches of Old Settlers* [Minnesota, 1886].

THE WILL[151]

My last will or testament at Prairie du Chien on the 22 day of january A. D. 1866.
In the name of the Blessed Trinity Father Son and Holy Ghost. I Lucien P.[?] M. Galtier born in St. Affrique Departmen of Aveiron in France now, in Prairie du Chien, Wisconsin in the U. S. do declare that the following lines are the expression of my free and last will or testament. In consequence, and in case of death, unless changed by another writing of mine, I by these do give and bequeath:

1st to the Right Revd. Bishop of Milwaukee for a permanent Catholic School conducted by the sisters of Benton[152] or some others if they refuse to accept, my brick house in Prairie du Chien together with the lot on which the same is built.

2nd every other lot or parcel of ground of which I have not disposed I likewise leave give and bequeath to the Rt. Revd. Bishop either for building some C. Church or to help the same aforesaid school.

3rd I give to the Seminary[153] my books, to the Church the whole of my church vestments with the exception of a double chasuble white and red another gold cloth. The two richest stoles as kept in a box and the two finest albs, which I leave for the use of my nephew, Lucien Galtier.

---

151 Using the spelling and punctuation of Father Galtier.
152 Benton, Wisconsin.
153 St. Francis Seminary of Milwaukee.

4ᵗʰ I give and bequeath to my Brother Eugène Galtier now in France, part of the property I have there at Maxillou that is to say the Chataigneraie partly planted with grape vines and east of Guibert ground. And I give and bequeath to my brother Louis Galtier the other part of the same property, that is, west of Guibert between Boulouis & my father's land, together with the house built on it.[154]

5ᵗʰ All monies due me and the amount now in my hands in all counting ten or nearly eleven thousand dollars I give them to my Sister Amelie Galtier in St. Affrique, with the express recommendation to her to have (365) masses three hundred and sixty five masses to be said for the rest of my soul and one hundred francs to be distributed to the poor as soon as she gets the aforesaid money.

6ᵗʰ I give and bequeath to my nephew Lucien, the small silver chalice and the big one guilt. (the new silver one belongs to the church) I give to him likewise my beautiful ivory statue valued (220 ff) two hundred and twenty francs my silver spoons cup & saucer, silver cruets & plate, forks, & knifes, and if he comes in Wisconsin—I give him a desk and sideboard (mahogany) a feather bed.
    I give to the Rt. Revd. Bishop of Milwaukee the painting of William Tell. All the others shall be left for my nephew if he comes here if not St. Vincent of Paul St. Francis of Paul are for the Church the others can be sold and their price used in paying the expenses of my burial as should be paid.
    The painting of Louis the 13ᵗʰ is worth (250 ff) two hundred and fifty francs, the others from 15 to 25. dollars each.
    The bureau with drawers (walnut) I give it to Mary Garvey—with the plates & dishes tumblers left empty. (The

---

154 Maxilou is a place near St. Affrique and Guibert and Boulouis are surnames of families that still exist in the area.

bedstead, a table & six chairs belong to the priest)[155]

The balance of funiture not specified can be given to Mrs. Mary Garvey together with her dues as it can be seen in my book-accounts.

There is in my room (327½) three hundred and twenty seven dollars and fifty cents in gold. Ninety dollars in silver (U.S.) and fifty francs in french gold.

In the hands of Mr. Famechon $7579.93) seven thousand five hundred & in the hands of Mr. Lawler--$2500, two thousand five hundred dollars.

    Mr. Manahan owes me $187.
    Mr. Foley...some other amount.
    Mr. Patrick Garvey $100.

I owe to Mary Garvey about $250 on the first of January 1866. To her brother on the 1st of February 1866 about $135.70. Then I keep in my bookcase on one of the shelfs

    for Mr. Lemieux forty dollars in currency
    for Mr. J. Coghland two hundred dollars
    for Mr. Gilmartin's sister one hundred dollars
    for Mr. Roche of the bluff ninety five dollars

& there is in my hands yet for the church from the old pew sold about sixty dollars.

My coffin should be common, my black vestment be used for the circumstances and no inscription but this pray for a sinner. My rest place should be near the front of the church outside.

[*Third, next, page is written for Father Galtier*]

    I hereby nominate and appoint H. L. Dousman, John Lawler and Barnaby Dunn all of Prairie du Chien the executors of this my last will and testament and hereby authorise and empower them the said H. L. Dousman, John Lawler and Barnaby Dunn[156] to compound, compromise and

---

155 That is, any priest who is serving St. Gabriel's.
156 John Lawler was a businessman and philanthropist and Barnaby Dunn [or Dunne] the Clerk of Crawford County. Both men were born in

settle any claim or demand which may be against or in favor of my said estate. In witness whereof I have hereunto set my hand seal this 21st of February AD 1866.

[*signature of Lucien Galtier*]

The above instrument consisting of two sheets was signed published and declared by the said testator to be his last will and testament in the presence of us who have signed our names at his request as witnesses in his presence and in presence of each other.

        O.B. Thomas Prairie du Chien Crawford Co. Wis.[157]
        J. Tilmont "   "
        J. Famechon "   "

Author's Note:
The following information from a French source very possibly pertains to Father Galtier, although the date of birth does not agree with that on the priest's tomb.

"Pierre Marie Lucien Galtier was born December 13, 1812. He was baptized on December 20. His parents were Antoine Jean Galtier and Angelique Raynal. They were married on June 6, 1802. Antoine Jean Galtier was the son of Stephen and Mary Durant Galtier, Saint Affrique. Angelique Raynal was the daughter of Pierre and Marie During Raynal of Saint Rome de Tarn."

    Ireland.
157 An attorney.

Tomb of Father Galtier, 1925

APPENDIX

Apart from letters, including those recollections sent to Bishop Grace, and the will, the author has not been able to discover anything written by Father Galtier except the following, which is, for some reason, a part of *Reminiscences, Memoirs, and Lectures of Monsignor A. Ravoux, V. G,* already cited. Certainly, there is some good advice imparted there but the biased viewpoint of woman as the ubiquitous temptress merely on account of her appearance and that sexual desires are somehow "corrupt" instead of quite natural detracts from any appeal the sermon might have to modern readers. Yet this is precisely the sort of homily one might have expected from a preacher, no matter what his denomination, in the 19th Century. The theater was also advised against as a source of possible moral degradation. In the midst of all this exaggerated dread of wrongdoing and guilt, the seeds of modern psychiatry were sown. Ironically, once the pendulum began to swing in the other direction, the world did not become a better place. Mankind, it would appear, has difficulty adhering for long to a moderate way of life, neither too prohibitive nor too permissive.

On Modesty, by Rev. Father L. Galtier who in 1841 Built the First Chapel in St. Paul and Died in Prairie du Chien in 1866—Modesty is a Virtue by which the Exterior is Regulated with Decorum and Decency—By it everything should be Ruled in our Exterior; our Eyes, our Tongue, our Dress and Manners.

"Let your modesty be known to all men: the Lord is nigh."--Phil.iv.5.

Beloved Christians:--It is the sacred task of the ministers of God to teach the faithful all their duties, even when they might have some reason to fear that many are not well disposed to receive with gratitude all the truths of salvation. "Preach the word," says St. Paul to his beloved disciple Timothy, "be instant in season, out of season, reprove, entreat, rebuke in all patience and doctrine." No less positive is the precept of our Saviour Jesus Christ when He gives command to His Apostles and their successors, to go and teach all nations, "Teaching them," says He, "to observe all things whatsoever I have commanded you, and behold I am with you, all days, even to the consummation of the world."

Were we only to please men of the world, we should never say a hard word against the feelings of corrupt nature. But we have to announce the doctrine of our blessed Lord, who, on many occasions, uttered the following anathema: "Woe to the world, because of scandals." Hence, we ought to arouse public attention, now and then, upon the multiplied abuses of society.

The subject of our instruction to-day, shall be Modesty.

Modesty, beloved faithful, is virtue by which the exterior is regulated with decency and decorum; by it, according to the example of Jesus Christ, everything should be properly ruled in our exterior, our eyes, our tongue, our dress and manners. Our eyes are, as it were, two windows, by which light or darkness is communicated to our soul; they may cause the fatal ruin of our heart, and be also to others an instrument of scandal.

Fully convinced of this truth was the holy patriarch Job, when he said: "I have made a covenant with my eyes, that I would not so much as to think upon a virgin."

Listen also to this advice of the Holy Ghost, by the mouth of Ecclesiasticus: "Gaze not upon a maiden, lest her beauty be a stumbling block to thee. Turn thy face from a woman dressed up, and gaze not upon another's beauty. For many have perished by the beauty of a woman and hereby lust is enkindled as a fire."

Be modest, watch and pray, if not, woe to you! Your eyes shall betray your heart and cause your ruin, according to these words of Jesus Christ: "I say to you that whosoever shall look on a woman to lust after her, hath already committed adultery with her in his heart."

These heavenly lessons are literally illustrated by two conspicuous examples read in the Holy Scripture. The first in the person of a great king and prophet, David, who, seduced by his imprudent looks at Urias' wife, became afterwards guilty of the double crime of adultery and murder. The second, no less remarkable, proves that old age itself is no guarantee, no security against such a disgraceful fall. Who has not heard the history of those two ancients, of those two judges of the people, who had free access to the house and orchard of Joakim, the spouse of chaste and virtuous Suzanna. Their immodest looks poisoned their hearts and plunged them into a abyss of iniquities; and because she feared God and would not give her consent, preferring death itself, she was accused by them before the people and condemned to die. But, glory to God! heaven could not see such abominable crimes on one side and such eminent virtue on the other, without taking hold of the curse and casting it upon the two monsters of iniquity, and at the same time delivering and crowning with glory Suzanna, the chaste wife, the perfect woman.

A third example of the danger caused by the immodesty of the eyes is likewise offered to the reflection of those who might think that the sex has nothing to fear from such imprudent wantonness. We read in Genesis that Putiphar's wife, having cast her eyes on Joseph, conceived such criminal passions in her heart that she forgot her rank, her duty, and used every means to bring the holy young man to a most horrible crime. But Joseph loved God and feared Him, and consequently preferred rather to expose himself to all kinds of sufferings in this life, than to offend Him.

Hence, to keep our hearts pure, we ought to pray and watch over our eyes and practice the virtue of modesty.

Our behavior and manners are also to be ruled by prudence and modesty. We must endeavor to let nothing indecent or light appear in our conduct. Gravity, candor, affability, kindness, ought to be the ornaments of our countenance, as they are the best marks of a good education and sound virtue.

Study, then, to be modest in all circumstances and in all places; with superiors because you owe them respect, and with equals and inferiors because you must give them edification and good example. Be modest, even when alone, on account of your guardian angel's presence, and more so of God, who sees all your actions.

"Let your modesty be known to all men; the Lord is nigh." This command of the Apostle ought to be chiefly understood of our behavior in the church, in the house of prayer, wherein is kept the tabernacle of the living God. "To enter the house of God as a profane house, without respect and modesty; gazing about, speaking without necessity, laughing; to be there in an unbecoming posture, lolling upon the seats, and other like irreverences, are sins which offend God," says a pious author, "more than the generality of people imagine."

Be modest and watch in the midst of your children; many times children have received at home, the first impressions of evil, and shall have to accuse, as murderers of their souls, the very authors of their life. Let your conduct be to them a continual lesson of modesty.

Allow in your house no immodest book or paper, no immodest painting or picture, no immodest statue–production of unchaste minds, so apt to convey the seed of corruption, the seed of moral and spiritual death, even in the most pure hearts. But have always for the use of your children and yourselves good books the reading of which will inspire them and you with good thoughts, good affections, good desires; adorn the walls of your rooms with paintings or pictures of Jesus Christ, of the blessed Virgin Mary, and other saints; the sight of which will convey to your minds lessons of modesty, purity, patience, and obedience to the will of God in all things.

Modesty regards dress also, wherein you must avoid superfluous ornaments, which are tokens of a vain and light mind, and dangerous to chaste eyes. Be modestly dressed or clothed, according to your condition and means, without trying to equal those who are far above you. "Glory not in apparel at any time," says the Holy Ghost, "for it is vain glory."

All the Fathers of the Church have strenuously condemned immodest dresses. St. Jerome calls young persons, who curl and trick up themselves wantonly, "the pest of modesty." And I do not find this holy Father too severe—when I read in the first Epistle of St. Paul to Timothy the following advice: "In like manner, women also in decent apparel: adorning themselves with modesty and sobriety, and not with plaited hair, or gold, or pearls, or costly attire, but as it becometh women professing godliness with good works."

To these words of St. Paul let me add also an advice of St. Peter, particularly addressed to married women: "Whose adorning," says the Prince of the Apostles, "let it not be the outward plaiting of the hair, or the wearing of gold, or the putting on of apparel, but the hidden man of the heart in the incorruptibility of a quiet and meek spirit, which is rich in the sight of God." O, beloved hearers, what a difference between the wise doctrine of the Apostles and that of the world!

Pagans and others, not followers of Jesus Christ, were extremely vain in their apparel, in their costly ornaments and immodest dresses, and this is the reason which induced St. Peter and St. Paul to forewarn Christians against scandals highly condemned by Jesus and His cross, in order to prevent amongst them contagion of so pernicious a custom, so bad an example. How much stronger would be their condemnation of such scandals, were these great Apostles amongst us witnessing the luxury, the vain attire, the indecent dressed, the light conduct and manners of so many followers of Christ of our days, who are ashamed to His cross and Christian modesty; of Christian modesty, which ought to be woman's greatest ornament, as also the glory and delight of all the disciples of Jesus Christ.

If you have a wise and regulated mind, it will appear by the modesty of your exterior, according to these words of the Holy Ghost: "A man is known by his looks, and a wise man, when thou meetest him, by his countenance. The attire of the body and the laughter of the teeth and the gait of a man shows what he is." Show what you are, but let it be by your modesty, by simple, humble and unassuming manners. Remember that the exterior is a copy of the interior, and the face, being the mirror of the soul, ought to be radiant with modesty. If you have a truly chaste heart and a real idea of virtue, you will despise all vain ornaments, all excess of attire as scandalous and ridiculous in Christians. Is it to reform God's own that you gather around your head so many trinkets and flowers? Do you not repudiate, by so many and so skillfully combined niceties, Jesus Christ, whose sacred head was crowned with thorns?

Observe modesty in your words, dearly beloved, for the wise man says, that "by the tongue wisdom is discerned."

Never speak a word ill or impertinent, but speak with wisdom and at a proper time. Never utter a wanton or indecent word, but edify others by your conversation. Avoid as a real plague, all unchaste discourses, the pest and corruption of good morals; do not use dubious expressions, expressions of double meaning, which might give occasion to evil thoughts. Shun all indecent language, all scurrilous words, which some sort of men, vulgar and mean, have frequently in their mouths. Besides, be discreet even on indifferent subjects; be the last in speaking and the first in holding silence, interrupting no one, meddling with no other's business. Learn before you speak, and always speak with a prudent forecast, and let circumspection, at all times, guide your lips.

These few remarks upon a matter of the greatest importance will induce you, I hope, to make some wholesome resolutions; and may the blessing of God reform your exterior, until you have acquired the modesty of the saints, together with their reward, the object of my wish unto you. In the name of the Father, *** Amen.

Alphabetical Index

A

Aldrich, Mrs. Mark, 88
Alim, Chief of the Fox, 132
Allcamp, 109
Allemann, Rev. John, 98, 103, 109-110, 112
143, 148, 152
American Fur Company, 35, 82
Anderson, Morgan (sheriff) 91
Ardèche, 15-16, 148
Astor, John Jacob, 35
Aveyron, 15-20

B

Badger (Dakota warrior) 30
Baker's settlement, 41
Barnabo, Cardinal Alessandro, 169
Barr, Dr. James, 183
Battle of Kaposia, 44-46, 63
Beaulieu, Josephine, 41
Beaumette, William, 40, 55
Becker, Rev. Peter, 189
Bedford, Barbara, 185
Bee Town, WI, 166
Belcourt, Rev. Georges, 144, 158
Big Thunder, Chief of the Dakota, 57
Black Hawk, Chief of the Sauk, 87, 135
Black Hawk War, 29, 86-87, 135
Black Robe, 9, 10
Black, Susan Easton, 94
Blanc, Bishop Anthony, 141, 142, 144, 146, 147
Blondeau, Maurice, 92
Blondeau, Pierre, 92
Boisvert, Antoine, 164
Bonduel, Rev. Florimond, 24-27, 106, 115, 128-131, 135,
139, 142, 156, 166
Booth, John Wilkes, 121
Boscobel, Wisconsin, 166

Bottineau, Charles, 63
Bottineau, Pierre, 63
Boucher, Françoise M., 41
Bourget, Bishop Ignatius, 144
Bowers, Faubion, 179
Boyd (mission), 169
Bras, Sr. Benvenuta, O.P., 22
Brattle, J.W., (surveyor of Keokuk) 93
Brigham Young University, 94
Brisbois, Michel, 134, 165
Brishnell, Edward, 93
Brown, Joseph R., 60
Brunelle, Louis, 41, 81
Burlington, Iowa, 87, 113
Burrall, Dr. F. A., 178-179
Busch, Rev. William, 162-63, 174, 185

C

California, 61, 147, 159-160
Campbell, Baptiste, 116, 119
Campbell, Henry J., 92, 93
Campbell, Hypolite, 119
Campbell, John, 120-121
Campbell, Joseph, 120
Campbell, Margaret, 35, 116, 121
Campbell, Mathias, 120
Campbell, Scott, 35, 44, 116, 120-121
Campbell, Scott, Jr., 120
Camp Coldwater, 42
Canada, 66
Carcassonne, France, 18
Cardinal, Genevieve, 41
Carnarvon, The Earl of, 179
Carver, Capt. Jonathan, 57-58, 132
Carver County, 79
Carver's Cave, 57
Cascade, Iowa, 103
Causse, Rev. Jacques, *arrival in America,* 22, 28; 43, 84, 104, 132, 138
Champagnie, Louis, 142
Chancery Office of Dubuque, 98
Chaska, Minnesota, 76
Cherrier, Denis, 40
Cherrier, Louis, 185

Chezard de Matel, Jeanne, 125
Chicago Diocese, 87, 143
Chippewa Indians, (see also Ojibway) 27, 30, 35, 44
Chippewa Language, 122
Chippewa Falls, Minnesota, 50, 65
cholera, 98, 128-129, 147
Cicero, 104
Cincinnati, Ohio Diocese, 169
Civil War, 6, 122
Clewett, James R., 40, 59-60
Coleman, Nancy, 96
Coleman, William, 96
Collins, Dr. F.M., 100
Columbus, Ohio Diocese, 172
Coryer, Albert, 166
Courier Press, 168
Crawford County, WI, 58, 132, 166, 171, 186
Cretin, Rev. Joseph, *arrival in America,* 22, 28; 74, 80, 84, 113, 114-15, 121, 125, 137, 142, 147, 152, 154-56 159-161, 169, 175
Crosby, Bing, 9

D

Dakota Indians, (see also Sioux) 10, 30, 32, 35, 44-46, 64, 121
Davenport, Iowa, 28, 86, 172
Dayton's Bluff, 57
De Cailly, Rev. Louis, 113, 169-170
De Forbin-Janson, Bishop, 52
de Galtier, Deodat, 18
de Galtier, Guillaume, 18
de Galtier, Pierre, 18
de Louis, Baron Henri, 91, 96
de Meersenhoven, Olisagers, 128, 131
Des Grieux, 24
Des Moines River, 87-88
Desoto (mission) 166
Detroit Diocese, 26
Devie, Bishop Alexande-Raymond (of Belley) 155
Dignan, Michael, 173
Dominicans, 98, 143
Dousman, H. Louis, 134, 135
Dousman, Hercules L., 132, 135, 139-140, 164, 186
Dousman Hotel, 165

Dousman, Jane, 132, 139-140, 165, 188
Dousman, Rosalie, 24-27, 106, 115
Do-wau ("The Singer") 58
Dubois, Antoine, 142
Dubourg, Bishop Louis, 82, 103
Dubuque, Iowa, 14, 42, 48, 74, 85, 87, 107, 113, 145
Dubuque Diocese, 22 et seq.
Ducharme, Desire, 185
Ducharme, Julie, 41
Dunand, Rev. Joseph, 189
Dunn, Barnaby, 186

E

Eastman, WI, 185
Ecclesiasticus, 28, 197
Eldred, Anson, 163
Emerson, Dr. J., 35, 37-39, 53
Emmitsburg, Maryland, 22
Emonds, Rev. Wilhelm, 122-123
Erdenberger, Charles, 165
Evans, William, 40

F

Famechon and Gaillard, 162, 182
Famechon, Jules, 162, 182, 186, 188, 194
Fanning, T., 96
Fargo, N. Dakota Diocese, 149
Faribault, Jean-Baptiste, 41, 49, 64, 65
Faribault family, 74, 79
Faribault, Minnesota, 119
Feddermann, Rev. Heinrich, 123
Fisher, Henry Munro, 133
Fitzpatric, Anne, 142
Flaget, Bishop Benedict Joseph, 109
Fleak, L.B., 107
Fond du Lac, Wisconsin, 173
Ford, Gov. Thomas, 94-95
Fort Atkinson, 170
Fort Crawford, 39, 134, 165
Fort Edwards, 88, 90, 98
Fort Madison, Iowa, 101-103, 110, 143, 170
Fort Shelby, 133-134
Fort Snelling, 31-40, 42, 44, 52, 53, 55, 99,

58, 81; *hospital*, 53-54; 134, 155, 158
Fountain Cave, 47, 48, 51, 54, 57
Fourviere, France, 126
Fox Indians, 132

G

Gagnier, Registre, 142
Gaillard, Auguste, 162, 182
Gaines, John, 87
Gaines, Mrs. John, 105, 107
Galena, Illinois, 28, 39, 87, 110, 135
Galland, Dr. Isaac, 87-88, 90-94, 97, 101, 107-109, 159-160
Galtier, Amilie, 187
Galtier, Eugene, 192
GALTIER, REV. LUCIEN, *origins*, 15-20;
on Protestant ministers, 9; arrival in America, 22;
relationship with Bishop Loras, 23-24;
coming to St. Peter's, 31-33; living at Mendota,42-48;
severe illness, 52-54; builds chapel of St. Paul,
61-64; *neighbors and flock, 65-66; Christmas of 1943 ,*
66-67; colleagues Ravoux and Godfert ,68-73;
dissatisfaction with Loras , 73-75; winter
of 1844, 78-79; leaving Minnesota, 80-83;
transfer to Keokuk, 84; impression on Virginia
Wilcox, 91; friendship with Dr. Galland, 92;
plans to build church, 95; working on the chapel,
96; wants to leave Keokuk, 103-107; argument with
Bishop Loras , 109-113; return to France, 114;
arrival at Prairie du Chien,132; debt of St. Gabriel's Church,
140; *plan to solicit donations in New Orleans, 141;*
Prairie du Chien and outlying missions, 162-171;
final days of Galtier, 172-189; summary of
Fr. Galtier's life, 189-190; Will, 191; Appendix and discourse
on modesty, 195-201.
Galtier, Louis [brother] 192
Galtier, Louis [actually Lucien, nephew], 171, 187
Gammel, François & fam., 45
Garvey, Mary, 188, 192, 193
Garvey, Patrick, 193
Gaud family, 18-19
Gautier de Verville, Madeleine, 133
Gear, Rev. Ezekiel, 39, 119
Gehl, Msgr. J. B., 27

Georgetown (mission) 169
Gervais, Alphonse, 58
Gervais, Bazille, 64
Gervais, Benjamin, 40, 51-52, 63
Gervais, Pierre, 40, 51-52, 63
Gilbraith, Major, 116
Godfert, Rev. Antoine, 66, 68-76, 79, 81, 82-85, 113, 114, 146, 167
Gokey [Gauthier] Phil, 176
Gonzega, Augustus, 90
Grace, Bishop Thomas, 161, 177
Graham, Duncan, 41
Green Bay, Wisconsin, 24-25, 137
Grey Cloud Island, 60
Guerin, Vital, 40, 51- 52, 59-61, 63, 154-155
Guildea, Hugh, 95, 99

H

Hains, Dr., 100
Hancock County, IL, 95
Hansen, Marcus L., 31
Hattenburger, Rev. Alexander, 143
Hays, John, 40, *murder of*, 56-58
Healy, Rev. John, 1143 144
Heiss, Bishop Michael, 165
Helvii (tribe) 18
Henni, Bishop John Martin, 80-81, 115, 129, 131, 139, 141, 142, 144, 146, 148, 165, 168, 170, 187
Henry of Navarre, 99
Hine, Daniel, 87, 88, 91
Hoffmann, Rev. Mathias M., 41, 48, 145
Hogan, "Dr.", 96, 106-107
Holy Cross, 109
Holy Ghost, 28, 183
Hood, Alex, 90
Hood, Louise, 89-91
Hooe, Capt. Alexander, 135
Hotel Rapids, 96
Hover, Dr., 100
Hudson, Minnesota, 65
Hughes, Katherine, 157
Hunt, Elizabeth, 90-91
Hutchinson, Minnesota, 118

I

Iowa City, Iowa, 114
Ireland, Bishop John, 15, 86, 127, 158, 167
Irish Ridge (mission) 166
Irvine, Cleopatra (Mrs. Richard Gorman) 65
Irvine, John (Mr. & Mrs.) 78
Ivins, Virginia (see also Wilcox) 88-89, 91, 92, 101, 104-106, 159-160
Ivins, William, 88, 159-160

J

Jackson, Henry, 63
Jarvis, Dr. Nathan, 37
Jenkins, Emily, 142
Jensen, Myra, 54
Jesuits, 9
Jewett family, 122
Johnson, _____, (settler at St. Peter's) 40
Johnson, Msgr. Peter Leo, 116
Johnston, Lyman, 89
Johnston, Sarah Marinda, 90
Juncker, Rev. Henry, 169

K

Kane's Hotel, 164
Kentucky, 50
Keokuk, Chief of the Sauk, 87, 91
Keokuk, Iowa, 80, 82, 85, 87-92, 95, 121, 124, 127, 132, 138, 150, 160, 166
Keokuk Medical College, 101
Keshena, Wisconsin, 24, 26, 107
Kickapoo mission, 166
Kickapoo River, 138
Kimmel Family, 170-171
Kimmel, John, 170-171
Klein, Robert, 22

L

Labershier, Frank, 93, 97 [real name "LaBuxiere"]
Labisonniere, Isaac, 46, 63
Labisonniere, Joseph, 63
LaBonne, Louis, 185

LaChappelle, Theophilus, 167
Lacombe, Rev. Albert, 157
LaCrosse, Wisconsin, 135, 166
LaCrosse Diocese, 165, 172, 165, 174, 189
Lake Harriet, 30
Lake Pepin, 66, 81
Lake Poygan, 26, 128, 131, 142
Lake St. Croix, 52
Lake Superior, 81
Languedoc, 17-19
LaRiviere, Alice, 185
LaRiviere, Pierre, 165
LaRiviere-Ravoux House, 175
Larpenteur, August, 79
Latourelle, Jean Baptiste, 41
Latter Day Saints (Mormons) 94
Lawler, John, 186, 193
Leblanc, Thomas, 135
LeClerc, Leander, 142
LeClere, Michel (or Leclaire) 41-42, 79
Le Conte, Joseph, 53-54
Lewis, Henry, 86
Liberty (mission) 166
Lincoln, Abraham, 121, 123
Lipcap, Solomon, 142
Little Canada, 65, 79
Little Crow, Chief of the Dakota, 45, 57, 116, 117-118, 120
Loras, Bishop Mathias, *left for America*, 21-22; *elevated to bishop*, 21; *arrival in New York with new missionaries*, 11, 15, 21-22; *at Fort Snelling*, 31, 38, 40-42; 48, 65, 66, 69, 70, 78, 80, 82-85, 86, 87, 96, 99, 102, 103, 106, 111, 113-115, 121, 123-124, 125-126, 137-137, 138, 139-140, 142, 143-147, 148, 151. 153, 156-157, 166, 170
Lord family, 44
Louis XIII, 186, 192
Louis IX, 17
Louisville, Kentucky, 110
Lyons, France, 21, 126, 170, 171

M

Mackinac Island, Michigan, 26 , 54, 135
Madelaine, Isabel, 41
Madison, Wisconsin, 132
Manahan, Benedict F., 136

Mankato, Minnesota, 117, 119
Manon (opera) 24
Mann, Sgt. (Fort Snelling) 38
Marietta, Ohio, 94
Marsh, Mr., 97
Marsh, L.R., 136
Martin, Angelique, 41
Martin, Louis, 41, 44
Mary Benedicta, O.P. (Sister) 29
Massac gang, 95
Massenet, Jules, 24
Massie's Landing, 42
Massif Central, 17
Maxilou, France, 192
Maynard, Louis, 167
Mazzuchelli, Rev. Samuel C., 9, 23, 27, 28-29, 84, 98, 109, 113, 115, 135-136, 143, 148, 150, 151, 154-155, 173
McBride, Alex, 93
McGregor, Iowa, 168, 181
McLeod, Penelope, 142, 167-168, 187-88
McDonald, Donald, 38
McNulty, Rev. Ambrose, 23, 63, 64
McPhail, James L., 180
Mechanic (steamboat) 92
Mendota, Minnesota (see also St. Peter's) 32-35, 41, 49, 50, 60, 64, 69, 78, 86, 147, 152-158, 173, 189
Menominee Indians, 26, 35, 108, 128
Methode Family, 142
metis, 35, 69
Meximieux Seminary, 22, 164
Michelet, Jules, 18
Mifflin (Iowa Country) 166
Milwaukee Diocese, 80 et seq., 165, 169, 187
Milwaukee, Wisconsin, 132
Mineral Point, 131
Mink (whiskey seller) 38
Minneapolis, Minnesota, 39
Minnehaha Falls, 30
Minnesota, 47, 55-56, 56, 64, 83, 107, 114, 117, 134-135, 148, 150, 151
Minnesota River (see also St. Peter River) 34
Mississippi River, 29-30, 39, 40 et seq.
Missouri River, 79, 138, 157, 165
Montpelier, France, 18

Morin, Amable, 41
Morin, François, 63
Mortimer, Sgt. Richard, 38, 78
Mousseau, Charles, 40
Mt. Hope, 169
Mt. Saint Bernard, 145
Muir, Dr. Samuel (surgeon at Fort Edwards) 89- 90
Muscoda (mission) 166
Myrick, Nathan, 132, 135

N

Narbonne, France, 17
Napoleon, 91
Nauvoo, Illinois, 94
New Orleans, LA., 128, 141, 142, 144
Newson, Thomas M., 20, 58, 64, 127, 157, 190
Nimes, France, 18
Notre Dame Sisters, 189

O

Ojibway Indians (see also Chippewa) 10, 30, 35, 40
"Old Bets", 45
Oshkosh, Chief of the Menominee, 106
Otting, Rev. Loras, 22
Ouanino, 41

P

Palean, Joshua, 93
Papin, (Pepin) Antoine, 44
Parrant, Pierre ("Pig's Eye") 38, 40, 48, 54-55, 79
Patch Grove, 138
Patten, Mrs. James, 38
Pelamourgues, Rev. Antoine, *arrival in America*, 22, 28; 41, 84, 137, 147, 169
Pembina, N. Dakota, 144, 163
Perrodin, Rev. Jean-Claude, 27, 137, 145, 157, 167, 173, 175
Perry, Abraham, 40, 61
Perry, Adele, 61
Petiot, Rev. Remigius, 22, 28, 84, 110, 138, 143
Petite Prairie, 78
Phelan, Edward, 40, 47, 51, 56-58, 59-61, 132
Philadelphia, PA, 93

Pigeon (mission) 166
Pig's Eye Landing, 16, 28, 34, 45, 63, 129
Pike Island, 39
Plympton, Maj. Joseph, 35, 37, 42, 43, 47
Pont d'Arc, 17
Pope Gregory XVI, 22, 88
Pope Pius IX, 165
Potawatamie, 93
Potosi, Wisconsin, 28-29, 109
Powers, Euphrosine, 135
Powers, Strange, 136
Poyet, Rev. Benoit, 146-147
Prairie du Chien, Wisconsin, 14, 51, 58, 69, 74, 128 et seq. 163 et seq.
Pritchard, Dr. L. W., 181
Provencher, Bishop, 65

Q

Quinn, Peter, 41, 44

R

Ramsey County, 61
"Rat Row", 88
Rattler, 45
Ravoux, Rev. Augustin, 11, *arrival in America,* 22, 28; 32, 55, 64, 65, 68-75, 76-79, 81, 82, 86, 113, 116, 120, 137, 147, 148, 150, 152, 156-158, 175, 195
Red River, 40, 51, 61, 163
Resche, Joseph, 44
Rhone River, 17
Robert, Louis, 81
Rodez, France, 15-18, 110, 112, 114, 115
Rolette, Emilie, 135
Rolette, Joseph, Sr., 132-134, 135, 139-140, 142, 164, 165
Rolette, Joseph, Jr., 134, 135
Rondeau, Joseph (Rondo) 40, 51
Rose, Violet, 185
Rosholt, Malcolm, 27
Rossico, Olivier, 41, 44
Rouergue, 16-17
Rum River, 31

S

St. Africanus, 20
St. Affrique, France, 16, 18, 20, 169, 187
St. Amant, Mme Marie Louise., 93
St. Andeol, 18
St. Anthony Falls, 66, 78, 156
St. Cessianus, 22
St. Clara Convent, Sisinawa, WI, 29
St. Croix, Minnesota, 30, 65, 66, 129, 156
St. Feriole Island, 164
St. Francis Seminary, 165, 191
St. Gabriel's Church, P. du Chien, 129, 135 et seq. 162 et seq.
St. Gaud, 18
St. Jacque, Julia, 176
St. Jacque, Louis, 171, 174-175, 176, 177, 180, 181, 184, 185, 186
St. Jacque, Rosina, 184, 185
St. Jacque, Toussaint, 176
St. Jerome, 199
St. John the Baptist mission, 166
St. John the Evangelist Church, Keokuk, 99, 115, 122
St. Joseph Academy, 128
St. Louis, Missouri, 82, 128, 135, 143
St, Louis Cathedral (New Orleans) 128, 142
St. Mark's chapel, 166
St. Paul (apostle) 178, 182
St. Paul Cathedral, 160
St. Paul Diocese, 147
St. Paul Pioneer Press, 69
St. Paul Seminary, 50, 147, 149
St. Paul's Chapel, St. Paul, 61-64, 153
St. Paul, Minnesota, 43, 46, 47, 50, 55,57, 58, 64, 65, 66, 80-82, 128-129, 130, 135, 138, 147, 152, 162, 164, 169
St. Peter (apostle) 199
St. Peter River (see also Minnesota River) 31, 40
St. Peter's (see also Mendota) 32-35, 42, 44, 53, 55, 58, 61, 66, 108, 130
St. Peter's Church, Mendota, 50, 65,
St. Peter's Church, Keokuk, 122
St. Philip's Church, Boyd, 166
St. Raphael's Church, Dubuque, 22
St. Stephen's Church, Richwoods, MO, 126

St. Vincent de Paul, 186, 192
Sanford, Dr. John F., 100
Santa Fe, New Mexico, 94
Sauk Indians, 135
Scanlan, Dr. Peter, 162-163, 177, 185
Scriabin, Alexander, 179-180, 184
Shakopee, Minnesota, 64
Shanty Town, 24
Siebauer, Rev. August, 173-174, 177
Sibley, Henry H., 58, 116, 117-118, 135
Sioux Indians (see also Dakota) 30-31, 35, 45, 119-121
Sioux language, 32, 69, 138
Sisters of the Incarnate Word, 125-126
Sisters of St. Joseph, 128
Skolla, Rev. Otto, 105-106
Smith, Lt. E.K., 42
Smith, Joseph, 94
Smyth, Dr. _____, 181, 183, 184
Snake Diggings (aka "Snake Hollow") 28
Snelling, Col. Josiah, 34
Society for the Propagation of the Faith (Lyons, France) 72, 75, 115, 118, 143, 145, 146, 172
Spruce Creek, 123
Stillwater, Minnesota, 64, 129-130
Sturgis, Nina, 135
Suydam, John, 115

T

Taliaferro, Maj. Lawrence, 35, 38, 56-57,
Taylor, Col. Zachary, 135, 165
Tell, William, 187, 192
Tilmont, J., 181, 183, 184, 188, 194
Toulouse, France, 109
Thebaud, Rev. Augustus, 50, 83
Thomas, O. B., 194
Traner Carriage Works, 164
Traverse des Sioux, 122
Trenerry, Walter N., 117
Turner, Dr. and Mrs., 52-54
Turpin, Amable, 44, 189
Turpin, Genevieve, 81
Treaties of 1837, 40

U
Utica (mission) 166

V
Valery, Jacques, 18
Valley, Antoine, 171
Vicaria Curiensis, 20
Villa Louis, 133, 164, 188
Villars, Rev. Jean, 97, 121-123
Visitation Convent, 121
voyageurs, 40, 60-61

W
Wabsheedah ("The Dancer") 57
Wahrheits Freund (newspaper) 40-41, 136
Warsaw, Illinois, 85, 97
Waterloo (mission) 166
West Point, 101, 103
Whipple, Bishop Henry, 119-120
Wilcox, Elizabeth, 95
Wilcox, Maj. John, 88, 90, 95
Wilcox, Virginia (see also Ivins) 190
Wild, John Casper, 39
Williams, J. Fletcher, 12, 40, 47, 58, 76
Winnebago, Indians, 114
Wisconsin River, 135, 137, 168
Wisconsin Territory, 58

Y
Yellow Medicine, Minnesota, 121

Z

www.ingramcontent.com/pod-product-compliance
Lightning Source LLC
Chambersburg PA
CBHW070548050426
42450CB00011B/2765